I0023545

THE 50 GREATEST SHARKS OF ALL TIME

VINCIT
OMNIA
VERITAS

☙ LOCHLAINN SEABROOK WRITES ACROSS THE FOLLOWING GENRES & TOPICS ❧

Academic
Acoustic Culture
Adventure
Aesthetics
Alternate History
American Civil War
American History
American Politics
American South
American West
Anatomy and Physiology
Ancient History
Animal Development
Antiquities
Anthologies
Anthropology
Apocrypha
Aquariology
Archaeology
Art
Art History
Astronomy
Aviation
Aviation History
Behavioral Science
Biblical Exegesis
Biblical Hermeneutics
Bioarchaeology
Biography
Book History
Botany
Camping
Children's Books
Children's Natural History
Christian Mysticism
Citizen's Rights Education
Civil Liberties
Civil Rights Law
Civil Self Defense
Clinical Studies
Coffee Table Books
Coloring Books
Comparative Aesthetics
Comparative Animal Development
Comparative History
Comparative Mythology
Comparative Religion
Conservation
Constitutional Law
Constitutional Studies
Cooking
Criminal Justice
Criminal Procedure
Cryptozoology
Cultural Anthropology
Cultural Geography
Cultural Heritage
Cultural Heritage Studies
Cultural History
Cultural Studies
Cultural Tourism
Deep Time Natural History
Destination Guides
Diet and Nutrition

Earth Sciences
Ecology
Ecotourism
Educational
Encyclopediography
Entertainment
Environmental History
Environmental Science
Environmental Studies
Environmental Tourism
Epistemology
Ethnobotany
Ethnology
Ethology
Ethnomusicology
Ethnic Studies
Etymology
European History
Evolutionary Anthropology
Evolutionary Biology
Evolutionary History
Evolutionary Psychology
Exploration
Exobiology
Exposes
Family Histories
Field Guides
Film
Folklore
Forestry
Genealogy
General Audience
Geography
Geology
Genetics
Ghost Stories
Gospels
Guidebooks
Handbooks
Health and Fitness
Heritage Conservation
Heritage Travel
Hiking
Historical Ecology
Historical Fiction
Historical Musicology
Historical Nonfiction
Historiography
History
History of Ideas
History of Medicine
History of Science
History of Technology
Hobbies and Crafts
Human-Animal Relationships
Human-Animal Studies
Human Evolution
Humanities
Humor
Ichthyology
Illustrated Lost History
Illustrated Music History
Illustrated Natural History
Illustrated Zoological Anthologies

Illustrations
Inspirational
Intellectual History
Interdisciplinary Lost Knowledge
Interviews
Journalism
Law Enforcement
Law of Attraction
Legal Studies
Lexicography
Life After Death
Life Stage Biology
Lifestyle
Literary History
Literature
Lost Intellectual Heritage
Lost Knowledge Studies
Lost Treasures
Marine Biology
Matriarchy
Medical History
Memoir
Men's Studies
Metahistory
Metaphysics
Military
Military History
Museum Studies
Music History
Musicology
Mysteries and Enigmas
Mysticism
Mythology
National Parks
Natural Health
Natural History
Natural Philosophy
Natural Science
Nature
Nature Appreciation
Nature Art
Nonfiction
Oceanography
Onomastics
Ontogeny
Outdoor Recreation
Paleoanthropology
Paleoecology
Paleography
Paleoichthyology
Paleontology
Paleozoology
Paranormal
Parapsychology
Parks & Campgrounds
Patriarchy
Patriarchy
Performing Arts
Philosophical Aesthetics
Philosophy
Philosophy of Science
Photography
Physical Anthropology
Pictorial

Poetry
Police Studies
Politics
Practical Law
Prehistoric Art
Prehistoric Life
Prehistory
Preservation Studies
Presidential History
Primatology
Primary Documents
Prophecy
Psychology
Public Safety
Quiz
Quotations
Recollections
Reference
Religion
Revolutionary Period
Science
Scripture
Self-help
Social Sciences
Sociology
Sound Studies
Southern Culture
Southern Heritage
Southern Narratives
Southern Studies
Southern Traditions
Speeches
Spirituality
Spiritualism
Sport Science
Symbolism
Technology
Thanatology
Thealogy
Theology
Theosophy
Tourism
Travel
UFOlogy
United States
Vanished Works Studies
Vexillology
Victorian Era Studies
Victorian Medicine
Visual Arts
Visual Cultural Memory Studies
Visual Encyclopediography
Visual Natural History
War
Western Art Music History
Western Civilization
Wildlife
Wildlife Biology
Wildlife Photography
Women's Studies
World History
Writing
Young Adult
Zoology

Mr. Seabrook does not author books for fame and glory, but for the love of writing and sharing his knowledge.

Be curious, not judgmental.

SeaRavenPress.com

Warning:
SEA RAVEN PRESS
BOOKS WILL EXPAND
YOUR ★ MIND!

The 50 Greatest

SHARKS OF ALL TIME

A Visual Guide to the Ocean's Apex Predators

LOCHLAINN SEABROOK

Bestselling Author, Award-winning Historian, Acclaimed Artist

Diligently Researched and Generously Illustrated by the Author for the Elucidation of the Reader

2025

Sea Raven Press, Park County, Wyoming, USA

THE 50 GREATEST SHARKS OF ALL TIME

Published by
Sea Raven Press, LLC, founded 1995
Park County, Wyoming, USA
SeaRavenPress.com

SEA RAVEN PRESS
Artisan-Crafted Books & Merch From the Rocky Mountains

All text, artwork, and illustrations copyright © Lochlainn Seabrook 2025
in accordance with U.S. and international copyright laws and regulations, as stated and protected under the Berne Union for the Protection of Literary and Artistic Property (Berne Convention), and the Universal Copyright Convention (the UCC). All rights reserved under the Pan-American and International Copyright Conventions.

PRINTING HISTORY
1st SRP paperback edition, 1st printing, October 2025 • ISBN: 978-1-955351-72-0
1st SRP hardcover edition, 1st printing, October 2025 • ISBN: 978-1-955351-73-7

ISBN: 978-1-955351-72-0 (paperback)
Library of Congress Control Number: 2026930107

This work is the copyrighted intellectual property of Lochlainn Seabrook and has been registered with the Copyright Office at the Library of Congress in Washington, D.C., USA. No part of this work (including text, covers, drawings, photos, illustrations, maps, images, diagrams, etc.), in whole or in part, may be used, reproduced, stored in a retrieval system, or transmitted, in any form or by any means now known or hereafter invented, without written permission from the publisher. The sale, duplication, hire, lending, copying, digitalization, or reproduction of this material, in any manner or form whatsoever, is also prohibited, and is a violation of federal, civil, and digital copyright law, which provides severe civil and criminal penalties for any violations.

The 50 Greatest Sharks of All Time: A Visual Guide to the Ocean's Apex Predators, by Lochlainn Seabrook. Includes an introduction, educational section, notes to the reader, and illustrations.

ARTWORK
Front and back cover design and art, book design, layout, font selection, and interior art by Lochlainn Seabrook.
All images, pictures, photos, illustrations, image captions, graphic design, and graphic art copyright © Lochlainn Seabrook.
All images created and/or selected, placed, manipulated, cleaned, colored, and tinted by Lochlainn Seabrook.
Cover image: "Carcharodon carcharias on the Hunt," copyright © Lochlainn Seabrook.
All rights reserved.

All persons who approve of the authority and principles of Colonel Lochlainn Seabrook's literary work, and realize its benefits as a means of reeducating the world about facts left out of mainstream books, are hereby requested to avidly recommend his titles to others and to vigorously cooperate in extending their reach, scope, and influence around the globe.

The views documented in this book concerning ichthyology, shark biology, and zoology are those of the publisher.

PROUDLY WRITTEN, DESIGNED, AND PUBLISHED, IN THE UNITED STATES OF AMERICA.

SHARK LIVES MATTER

Dedication

TO THE LEMON SHARK

One morning, while snorkeling off the coast of Palm Beach County, Florida, I was aggressively bluff charged by an eight-foot, 250-pound member of this species. Staring into the tooth-filled mouth of that underwater giant, I knew my life hung in the balance. Yet, as a naturalist, my only thought at the time was how extraordinarily perfect it was—the sleek lines, the hydrodynamic contours, the fin placement, the gill design, the coloring, the flawless symmetry.

I managed to survive the harrowing encounter. And though it occurred long ago, one realization has remained with me through all of the intervening years: Sharks are biological masterpieces, living works of art that combine both grace and power, beauty and efficiency. They are, in short, the absolute pinnacle of evolutionary design, making them the undisputed masters of their realm. L.S.

Lemon Shark (*Negaprion brevirostris*). Copyright © Lochlainn Seabrook.

Epigraph

Think we don't need sharks? If every species vanished tomorrow, what's known as a trophic collapse would begin instantly—a catastrophic chain reaction rippling through every ecosystem on Earth. Climate and oxygen levels would shift, food chains would disintegrate, and global biodiversity would plummet. In time, under the weight of these profound disruptions, the seas would die, our planet would become uninhabitable, and humankind itself would face extinction.

Lochlainn Seabrook, 2025

Shortfin Mako (*Isurus oxyrinchus*). Copyright © Lochlainn Seabrook.

CONTENTS

Notes to the Reader ❧ page 11
Why We Need Sharks, by Lochlainn Seabrook ❧ page 12
Introduction, by Lochlainn Seabrook ❧ page 13

1. Angelshark (*Squatina squatina*) ❧ page 16
2. Basking Shark (*Cetorhinus maximus*) ❧ page 18
3. Bigeye Thresher (*Alopias superciliosus*) ❧ page 20
4. Blacktip Shark (*Carcharhinus limbatus*) ❧ page 22
5. Blue Shark (*Prionace glauca*) ❧ page 24
6. Bonnethead Shark (*Sphyrna tiburo*) ❧ page 26
7. Broadnose Sevengill Shark (*Notorynchus cepedianus*) ❧ page 28
8. Bull Shark (*Carcharhinus leucas*) ❧ page 30
9. Cladoselache (*Cladoselache fyleri*) ❧ page 32
10. Cookiecutter Shark (*Isistius brasiliensis*) ❧ page 34
11. Epaulette Shark (*Hemiscyllium ocellatum*) ❧ page 36
12. Frilled Shark (*Chlamydoselachus anguineus*) ❧ page 38
13. Galapagos Shark (*Carcharhinus galapagensis*) ❧ page 40
14. Ganges Shark (*Glyphis gangeticus*) ❧ page 42
15. Ginsu Shark (*Cretoxyrhina mantelli*) ❧ page 44
16. Goblin Shark (*Mitsukurina owstoni*) ❧ page 46
17. Great Hammerhead (*Sphyrna mokarran*) ❧ page 48
18. Great White Shark (*Carcharodon carcharias*) ❧ page 50
19. Greenland Shark (*Somniosus microcephalus*) ❧ page 52
20. Horn Shark (*Heterodontus francisci*) ❧ page 54
21. Japanese Sawshark (*Pristiophorus japonicus*) ❧ page 56
22. Kitefin Shark (*Dalatias licha*) ❧ page 58
23. Lemon Shark (*Negaprion brevirostris*) ❧ page 60
24. Leopard Shark (*Triakis semifasciata*) ❧ page 62
25. Longfin Mako (*Isurus paucus*) ❧ page 64
26. Megalodon (*Otodus megalodon*) ❧ page 66
27. Megamouth Shark (*Megachasma pelagios*) ❧ page 68
28. Nurse Shark (*Ginglymostoma cirratum*) ❧ page 70
29. Oceanic Whitetip Shark (*Carcharhinus longimanus*) ❧ page 72
30. Ornate Wobbegong (*Orectolobus ornatus*) ❧ page 74
31. Porbeagle (*Lamna nasus*) ❧ page 76
32. Sandbar Shark (*Carcharhinus plumbeus*) ❧ page 78
33. Sand Tiger Shark (*Carcharias taurus*) ❧ page 80
34. Scalloped Hammerhead (*Sphyrna lewini*) ❧ page 82
35. Scissor-Tooth Shark (*Edestus giganteus*) ❧ page 84
36. Sharpnose Sevengill Shark (*Heptranchias perlo*) ❧ page 86

37. Shortfin Mako (*Isurus oxyrinchus*) ❧ page 88
38. Silky Shark (*Carcharhinus falciformis*) ❧ page 90
39. Small-spotted Catshark (*Scyliorhinus canicula*) ❧ page 92
40. Smoothhound Shark (*Mustelus mustelus*) ❧ page 94
41. Spiny Dogfish (*Squalus acanthias*) ❧ page 96
42. Spotted Wobbegong (*Orectolobus maculatus*) ❧ page 98
43. Squalicorax (*Squalicorax pristodontus*) ❧ page 100
44. Stethacanthus (*Stethacanthus altonensis*) ❧ page 102
45. Swell Shark (*Cephaloscyllium ventriosum*) ❧ page 104
46. Thresher Shark (*Alopias vulpinus*) ❧ page 106
47. Tiger Shark (*Galeocerdo cuvier*) ❧ page 108
48. Velvet Belly Lanternshark (*Etmopterus spinax*) ❧ page 110
49. Whale Shark (*Rhincodon typus*) ❧ page 112
50. Zebra Shark (*Stegostoma tigrinum*) ❧ page 114

Meet the Author-Historian-Artist ❧ page 117
Praise for the Author ❧ page 119
Learn More ❧ page 123

Zebra shark (*Stegostoma tigrinum*). Copyright © Lochlainn Seabrook.

NOTES TO THE READER

MY SOURCES
☞ As with all of my natural history books, every effort has been made to present the latest reliable data available, free of bias and speculation.

MY RESEARCH
☞ Due to the difficulties inherent in oceanography, ichthyology, paleoichthyology, marine biology, and limnology, scientific consensus is not always possible. As such, my research may differ from that of other nature writers, and in particular various fish researchers and marine scientists. In some cases certain data are estimated.

CONSERVATION STATUS
☞ I use the IUCN's (International Union for Conservation of Nature) nine-category Red List classification system.

Blue shark (*Prionace glauca*). Copyright © Lochlainn Seabrook.

Why We Need Sharks

Sharks are essential to maintaining the health of the oceans and, by extension, all life on Earth. As apex predators that have existed for nearly a half billion years, they play a crucial role in keeping marine ecosystems balanced, productive, and resilient. Their influence extends far beyond the sea, supporting biodiversity, regulating climate systems, and even aiding human industries and medicine.

KEY WAYS SHARKS BENEFIT THE PLANET AND HUMANITY

- Maintain Marine Balance: Sharks regulate populations of fish and other marine species, preventing overpopulation and ensuring ecological stability.
- Promote Genetic Health: By preying on the weak, sick, and old, sharks strengthen gene pools and sustain healthy, resilient populations.
- Protect Coral Reefs: Sharks keep mid-level predators in check, allowing smaller herbivorous fish to thrive and control algae that would otherwise smother coral reefs.
- Preserve Seagrass Meadows: By managing populations of grazers such as turtles and dugongs, sharks safeguard vast seagrass ecosystems that store massive amounts of "blue carbon."
- Combat Climate Change: Healthy shark populations help maintain oceanic carbon sinks—coral reefs and seagrass beds—that absorb and store atmospheric carbon dioxide.
- Support Biodiversity: As keystone species, sharks influence nearly every level of the marine food web, helping to sustain diverse ocean life.
- Prevent Disease Outbreaks: By removing weak or infected individuals from fish populations, sharks reduce the spread of disease in marine environments.
- Boost Coastal Protection: Healthy coral reefs supported by shark activity protect shorelines from erosion and storm surges.
- Sustain Human Livelihoods: Sharks help maintain fish stocks vital for global food security and sustainable fisheries.
- Drive Ecotourism: Shark diving and observation industries generate millions of dollars annually, providing long-term economic benefits to coastal communities.
- Advance Medical Research: Studies of shark biology have inspired breakthroughs in wound healing, cancer resistance, and immune system science.
- Preserve Ocean Oxygen Production: By maintaining marine ecosystem balance, sharks indirectly support the phytoplankton that produce most of Earth's oxygen.
- Promote Planetary Health: A thriving shark population is an indicator of a healthy ocean—vital for regulating climate, producing oxygen, and supporting life on Earth. By keeping the oceans in balance, sharks help sustain the planetary systems that make human life possible.

INTRODUCTION

FOR MORE THAN 400 million years, sharks have ruled the world's oceans. They are among the oldest surviving vertebrates on Earth—apex predators whose lineage predates dinosaurs, trees, and even flowering plants. Perfected by time, they have evolved into forms so efficient that little about them has needed to change. From the graceful movements of today's blue shark to the armored bulk of the ancient *Cladoselache*, each species represents a triumph of natural design.

My book, *The 50 Greatest Sharks of All Time*, is both a celebration and an exploration of that design. Here, readers will encounter the giants of prehistory alongside the sleek hunters of today. Some are familiar names—the great white, the tiger, the hammerhead—while others, like *Stethacanthus* and *Edestus*, belong to a vanished world that can now only be glimpsed through fossilized remains. Together, they form a panoramic portrait of evolution's most enduring success story: the shark!

Silky Shark (*Carcharhinus falciformis*). Copyright © Lochlainn Seabrook.

To observe a shark is to witness the intersection of power and elegance. Every contour serves a purpose; every movement conserves energy. Their sensory systems border on the miraculous, capable of detecting the faintest electrical impulses of distant prey. Their hydrodynamic bodies, so finely tuned, demonstrate that in the natural world beauty and function often appear together.

As both a naturalist and lifelong student of marine life, I have spent decades both studying and swimming with these extraordinary animals. What follows is not merely a catalog of species, but a personal guided journey through time and adaptation—from the primordial seas of the Devonian to the living reefs of the modern world.

May these pages broaden your view of sharks as vital architects of the ocean's balance, symbols of nature's boundless creativity, and indispensable strands in the web of life. They are in the truest sense of the word, marvels of survival, and deserve our respect.

Lochlainn Seabrook
Park County, Wyoming USA
October 2025

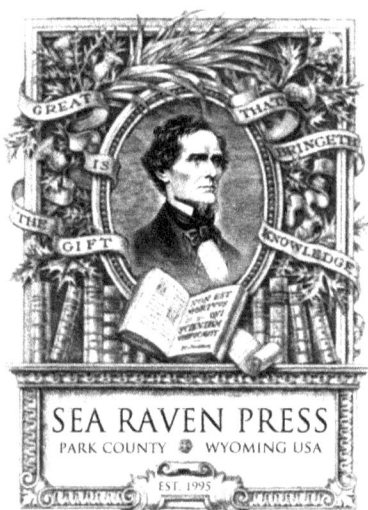

SEA RAVEN PRESS
PARK COUNTY ❦ WYOMING USA
EST. 1995

"Books invite all; they constrain none."
Hartley Burr Alexander (1873-1939)

The 50 Greatest

SHARKS

of All Time

ANGELSHARK

COMMON NAME: Angelshark.
SCIENTIFIC NAME: *Squatina squatina* (Linnaeus, 1758).
FAMILY: Squatinidae.
GROUP: Angelsharks.
BIOLOGICAL STATUS: Living.
TIME ON EARTH: About 150 million years.
GEOLOGIC AGE: Late Jurassic to present.
SIZE: Up to 8 ft long; average 5 ft; females up to 175 lb.
HABITAT: Coastal continental shelves and sandy seabeds.
DEPTH RANGE: Shallow water to about 500 ft.
GEOGRAPHIC RANGE: Eastern Atlantic from Norway to North Africa; Mediterranean Sea.
DIET: Bottom fish, crustaceans, and mollusks.
DISTINGUISHING FEATURES: Flattened body with winglike pectoral fins; eyes on top of head; mottled brown or gray coloration for camouflage.
ANATOMY & ADAPTATIONS: Ray-like body allows concealment under sand. Eyes and spiracles positioned for ambush hunting. Jaws project forward rapidly to seize prey. Rough skin and cryptic coloring provide protection. Broad pectorals generate lift near the seafloor. Lateral line detects vibrations from buried prey.
BEHAVIOR: Nocturnal ambush predator. By day it buries in sediment; at night it hunts along the bottom. Capable of short bursts up to 15 mph when attacking or escaping. Generally motionless unless disturbed. Occasionally emits a barklike sound when provoked or handled. Moves with slow undulations when gliding over the seabed.
REPRODUCTION: Ovoviviparous with litters of 7–25 pups. Gestation about 8–10 months. Newborns measure around 10 inches.
PREDATORS: Large sharks, monk seals, and humans.
DANGER TO HUMANS: Generally harmless. Bites only when stepped on or handled; incidents are rare and minor.
CONSERVATION STATUS: "Critically Endangered." Nearly eradicated by bycatch, habitat loss, and trawl fishing; now confined mainly to waters near the Canary Islands and southern Europe.
NOTABLE FACTS: Common in European waters until the 20th Century. Its flattened shape led to frequent misidentification as a ray. Now one of the rarest sharks in the eastern Atlantic and a focus of ongoing recovery efforts by regional conservation programs.

Angelshark, *Squatina squatina*. Copyright © Lochlainn Seabrook.

BASKING SHARK

COMMON NAME: Basking shark.
SCIENTIFIC NAME: *Cetorhinus maximus* (Gunnerus, 1765).
FAMILY: Cetorhinidae.
GROUP: Mackerel sharks.
BIOLOGICAL STATUS: Living.
TIME ON EARTH: About 30 million years.
GEOLOGIC AGE: Oligocene to present.
SIZE: Up to 40 ft long; average 25–30 ft; up to 8 tons.
HABITAT: Coastal and open-ocean waters of temperate regions.
DEPTH RANGE: Surface to about 3,000 ft.
GEOGRAPHIC RANGE: Widely distributed in both hemispheres; common in the North Atlantic, North Pacific, and southern temperate coasts.
DIET: Zooplankton, small crustaceans, and fish larvae.
DISTINGUISHING FEATURES: Massive size; wide gaping mouth; conical snout; long gill slits encircling the head; tall, triangular dorsal fin.
ANATOMY & ADAPTATIONS: Filter-feeding giant with gill rakers that trap microscopic prey. Large liver provides buoyancy. Skin covered in coarse denticles reduces drag. Slow metabolism suits cold, nutrient-rich waters. Countershading aids concealment.
BEHAVIOR: Slow, non-aggressive swimmer that cruises near the surface in small groups. Normal speed about 2 mph with bursts up to 6 mph. Often seen feeding with mouth open, filtering hundreds of gallons of water per hour. Migrates seasonally following plankton blooms. Occasionally breaches or swims vertically while feeding. Sometimes basks motionless at the surface.
REPRODUCTION: Ovoviviparous. Gestation likely exceeds 2 years. Produces litters of 4–6 pups, each 5–6 ft long at birth.
PREDATORS: Great white sharks, orcas, and humans.
DANGER TO HUMANS: Harmless. Gentle nature and filter-feeding diet make it no threat to swimmers or divers.
CONSERVATION STATUS: "Endangered." Severely depleted by historical hunting for oil and fins; recovery slow due to late maturity and low reproductive rate.
NOTABLE FACTS: Second largest fish on Earth after the whale shark. Despite its size, peaceful and docile. Sometimes mistaken for great whites when dorsal and tail fins break the surface. Often seen in plankton-rich coastal waters during summer months and now protected in many regions.

Basking shark, *Cetorhinus maximus*. Copyright © Lochlainn Seabrook.

BIGEYE THRESHER

COMMON NAME: Bigeye thresher.
SCIENTIFIC NAME: *Alopias superciliosus* (Lowe, 1841).
FAMILY: Alopiidae.
GROUP: Thresher sharks.
BIOLOGICAL STATUS: Living.
TIME ON EARTH: About 23 million years.
GEOLOGIC AGE: Miocene to present.
SIZE: Up to 20 ft long including tail; body 11 ft; up to 350 lb.
HABITAT: Deep offshore waters and continental slopes.
DEPTH RANGE: Surface to about 1,600 ft.
GEOGRAPHIC RANGE: Circumtropical and temperate oceans worldwide. Common in the Atlantic, Pacific, and Indian Oceans.
DIET: Small schooling fish, squid, and crustaceans.
DISTINGUISHING FEATURES: Huge upper tail lobe equal to body length; large upward-directed eyes; short snout; sleek, metallic-gray body fading to pale underside.
ANATOMY & ADAPTATIONS: Tail used as a whip to stun prey. Large eyes adapted for low light in deep water; capable of rotating upward to track prey above. Long pectoral fins provide lift during slow swimming. Small mouth with sharp teeth for grasping prey. Streamlined body minimizes drag. Heat-retaining blood vessels conserve muscle warmth at depth.
BEHAVIOR: Solitary hunter that feeds mainly at night. Circles schools of fish and strikes with tail to disable prey. Normal speed about 3–4 mph with bursts over 20 mph when attacking. Performs daily vertical migrations between surface and deep zones. Occasionally leaps clear of the water when pursued or hooked.
REPRODUCTION: Ovoviviparous with litters of 2–4 pups. Embryos feed on unfertilized eggs inside the uterus. Pups born around 5 ft long. Maturity reached near 12 years.
PREDATORS: Larger sharks and killer whales; humans are primary threat.
DANGER TO HUMANS: Generally harmless. Avoids divers; may thrash with tail if caught or provoked.
CONSERVATION STATUS: "Vulnerable." Declining due to bycatch and demand for fins and meat. Slow reproduction limits recovery.
NOTABLE FACTS: One of the few sharks that uses its tail as a weapon. Large eyes give it excellent vision in dim light. Often mistaken for the common thresher.

Bigeye thresher, *Alopias superciliosus.* Copyright © Lochlainn Seabrook.

BLACKTIP SHARK

COMMON NAME: Blacktip shark.
SCIENTIFIC NAME: *Carcharhinus limbatus* (Müller and Henle, 1839)
FAMILY: Carcharhinidae.
GROUP: Requiem sharks.
BIOLOGICAL STATUS: Living.
TIME ON EARTH: About 23 million years.
GEOLOGIC AGE: Miocene to present.
SIZE: Up to 8 ft long; average 5–6 ft; up to 150 lb.
HABITAT: Coastal and offshore tropical and subtropical waters.
DEPTH RANGE: Surface to about 500 ft.
GEOGRAPHIC RANGE: Worldwide in warm seas; common in the western Atlantic, Gulf of America, Caribbean, and Indo-Pacific.
DIET: Small schooling fish, cephalopods, and crustaceans.
DISTINGUISHING FEATURES: Slender body with pointed snout; black tips on fins; bronze-gray upper surface and white underside; strongly forked tail.
ANATOMY & ADAPTATIONS: Streamlined body enables rapid pursuit of prey. Sharp triangular teeth suited for cutting small fish. Keen eyesight detects flashes of schooling prey. Countershading provides camouflage. Strong caudal fin supplies thrust for fast acceleration. Electroreceptors detect faint electrical fields.
BEHAVIOR: Active, fast-swimming predator. Often forms feeding groups around baitfish. Frequently leaps from the water while hunting. Normal speed about 6 mph with bursts over 20 mph. Migrates seasonally following warm currents and prey. Rarely aggressive unless provoked or feeding. Commonly seen near reefs, estuaries, and coastal drop-offs.
REPRODUCTION: Viviparous. Gestation 10–12 months. Litter size 4–10 pups, each about 20 inches at birth. Uses coastal nursery areas in shallow water.
PREDATORS: Larger sharks and humans.
DANGER TO HUMANS: Moderate. Responsible for occasional non-fatal bites, usually involving fishing or feeding events. Avoids direct contact with swimmers.
CONSERVATION STATUS: "Near Threatened." Declines due to overfishing, bycatch, and habitat loss in nursery zones.
NOTABLE FACTS: Often confused with the spinner shark. Known for its spectacular spinning leaps when chasing prey. Plays an important ecological role in maintaining balanced fish populations.

Blacktip shark, *Carcharhinus limbatus*. Copyright © Lochlainn Seabrook.

BLUE SHARK

COMMON NAME: Blue shark.
SCIENTIFIC NAME: *Prionace glauca* (Linnaeus, 1758).
FAMILY: Carcharhinidae.
GROUP: Requiem sharks.
BIOLOGICAL STATUS: Living.
TIME ON EARTH: About 20 million years.
GEOLOGIC AGE: Miocene to present.
SIZE: Up to 12.5 ft long; average 6–10 ft; up to 250 lb.
HABITAT: Open ocean, mainly near the surface in temperate and tropical waters.
DEPTH RANGE: Surface to about 1,150 ft.
GEOGRAPHIC RANGE: Cosmopolitan; offshore waters of all major oceans from 60° N to 50° S.
DIET: Small fish, squid, and crustaceans.
DISTINGUISHING FEATURES: Slender, elongated body; long pectoral fins; narrow pointed snout; deep blue back fading to pale sides and white belly.
ANATOMY & ADAPTATIONS: Streamlined body built for endurance. Long fins provide lift and stability. Countershading conceals the shark in open water. Serrated teeth grasp slippery prey. High red-muscle content improves stamina for migration. Large gill surface supports continuous swimming.
BEHAVIOR: Highly migratory and social. Often forms groups by size and sex. Normal speed about 3 mph with bursts up to 43 mph. Constant swimmer that must move to breathe. Curious toward divers but rarely aggressive. Hunts mainly at night near the surface. Frequently circles boats while investigating new objects.
REPRODUCTION: Viviparous. Gestation 9–12 months. Litters of 25–50 pups, each 15–20 inches at birth. Maturity reached around 5–6 years.
PREDATORS: Larger sharks, killer whales, and humans.
DANGER TO HUMANS: Low. Generally shy; few confirmed attacks, usually related to feeding events.
CONSERVATION STATUS: "Near Threatened." Declining from longline bycatch and fin trade. Slow growth and low recovery rates.
NOTABLE FACTS: Among the most wide-ranging sharks. Known for graceful movement and long transoceanic migrations. Plays an important role in regulating mid-ocean prey populations. Sometimes follows ships for long distances, feeding on discarded catch. May travel thousands of miles between feeding grounds.

Blue shark, *Prionace glauca*. Copyright © Lochlainn Seabrook.

BONNETHEAD SHARK

COMMON NAME: Bonnethead shark.
SCIENTIFIC NAME: *Sphyrna tiburo* (Linnaeus, 1758).
FAMILY: Sphyrnidae.
GROUP: Hammerhead sharks.
BIOLOGICAL STATUS: Living.
TIME ON EARTH: About 20 million years.
GEOLOGIC AGE: Miocene to present.
SIZE: Up to 5 ft long; average 3–4 ft; up to 24 lb.
HABITAT: Shallow coastal waters, bays, and estuaries.
DEPTH RANGE: Surface to about 260 ft.
GEOGRAPHIC RANGE: Western Atlantic from New England to Brazil; eastern Pacific from southern California to Ecuador; common in the Gulf of America and Caribbean.
DIET: Crustaceans, small fish, mollusks, and seagrass.
DISTINGUISHING FEATURES: Small hammer-shaped head with rounded lobes; gray to olive upper body with pale underside; slender build and short snout.
ANATOMY & ADAPTATIONS: Distinct cephalofoil enhances sensory range and maneuverability. Ampullae of Lorenzini detect prey buried in sand. Flat teeth crush shellfish. Intestine adapted for partial herbivory—the only shark known to digest plant matter. Streamlined body reduces drag. Large dorsal fin stabilizes turns in shallow water.
BEHAVIOR: Active, social species often found in small groups. Swims continuously at a steady pace around 2–3 mph. Migrates seasonally to warmer regions. Feeds by rooting in sand and snapping up prey. Dives to moderate depths during temperature shifts. Exhibits schooling behavior for protection.
REPRODUCTION: Viviparous. Gestation 4–5 months. Litters of 4–16 pups about 12 inches long at birth. Maturity reached around 2 years.
PREDATORS: Larger sharks and humans.
DANGER TO HUMANS: Harmless. Too small to pose a threat; avoids swimmers.
CONSERVATION STATUS: "Least Concern," though regional declines reported from overfishing and habitat degradation.
NOTABLE FACTS: Only known omnivorous shark species. Uses head shape to pin down prey. Often seen cruising nearshore grass beds in daylight. Highly tolerant of brackish waters and temperature variation.

Bonnethead shark, *Sphyrna tiburo*. Copyright © Lochlainn Seabrook.

BROADNOSE SEVENGILL SHARK

COMMON NAME: Broadnose sevengill shark.

SCIENTIFIC NAME: *Notorynchus cepedianus* (Péron, 1807).

FAMILY: Hexanchidae.

GROUP: Cow sharks.

BIOLOGICAL STATUS: Living.

TIME ON EARTH: About 200 million years.

GEOLOGIC AGE: Late Triassic to present.

SIZE: Commonly 9–10 ft long; up to 11 ft; weight 200–400 lb.

HABITAT: Coastal and continental shelf waters, bays, and estuaries.

DEPTH RANGE: Surface to roughly 450 ft.

GEOGRAPHIC RANGE: Temperate regions of the Atlantic, Pacific, and Indian Oceans, including California, South Africa, southern Australia, Japan, and Chile.

DIET: Opportunistic predator feeding on fish, rays, sharks, seals, and carrion.

DISTINGUISHING FEATURES: Broad, blunt snout; single dorsal fin far back on body; seven gill slits instead of the typical five; small eyes; heavy, mottled gray body with lighter underside.

ANATOMY & ADAPTATIONS: Possesses saw-like lower teeth for cutting large prey; flexible body for rapid turning; electroreceptive organs for locating hidden animals; powerful jaws for scavenging and predation; large liver for buoyancy control.

BEHAVIOR: Mostly nocturnal hunter, often cruises near the bottom or enters shallow bays at night. Forms loose feeding groups around seal colonies. Swims steadily at about 3–5 mph but can lunge quickly when attacking.

REPRODUCTION: Ovoviviparous. Females produce litters of 60–100 pups after a gestation of about one year.

PREDATORS: Larger sharks, including great whites and tiger sharks, and orcas.

DANGER TO HUMANS: Considered potentially dangerous; rare attacks reported, usually provoked or during spearfishing.

CONSERVATION STATUS: "Vulnerable" due to coastal habitat loss and overfishing.

NOTABLE FACTS: This ancient species is the only living member of its genus, linking modern sharks to their Jurassic ancestors. Known as a "living fossil," it retains primitive features found in ancient sharks. Commonly seen in South Africa's False Bay. Sometimes called the "Cow Shark of the Deep." Found to hunt cooperatively when targeting large prey.

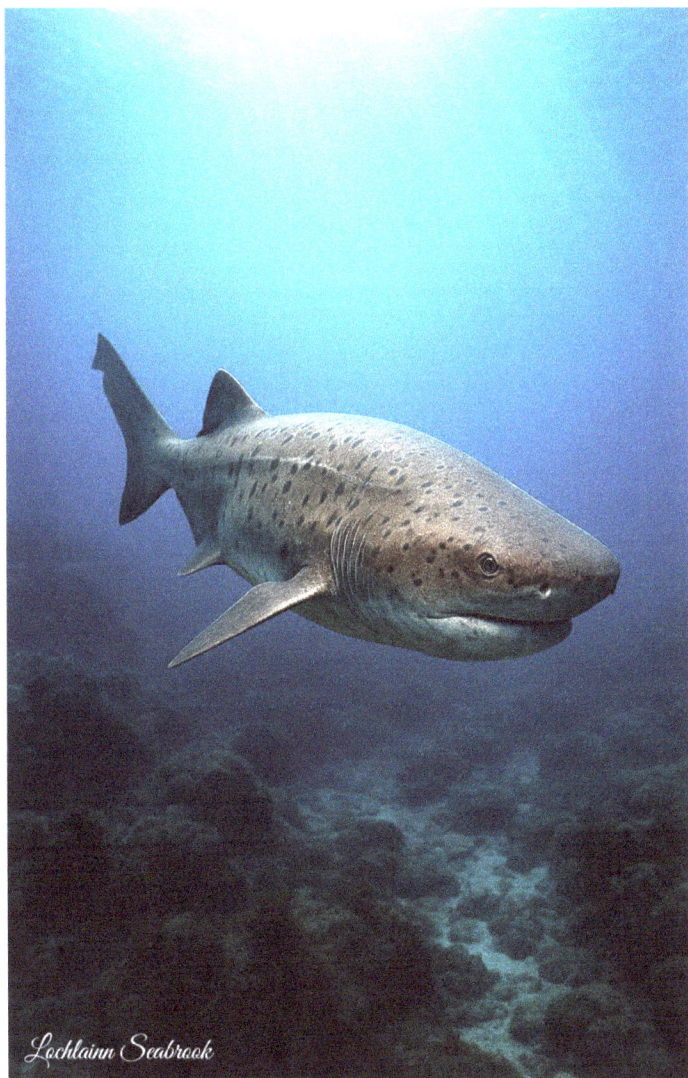

Broadnose sevengill shark, *Notorynchus cepedianus*. Copyright © Lochlainn Seabrook.

BULL SHARK

COMMON NAME: Bull shark.
SCIENTIFIC NAME: *Carcharhinus leucas* (Valenciennes, 1839).
FAMILY: Carcharhinidae.
GROUP: Requiem sharks.
BIOLOGICAL STATUS: Living.
TIME ON EARTH: Since the Miocene Epoch, about 16 million years.
GEOLOGIC AGE: Neogene Period.
SIZE: Average 7.5 ft; large females to 11.5 ft; weight 200–900 lb.
HABITAT: Coastal marine and freshwater environments including rivers, estuaries, and lakes.
DEPTH RANGE: Surface to 500 ft.
GEOGRAPHIC RANGE: Tropical and subtropical waters worldwide; common in the Atlantic, Indian, and Pacific Oceans, and major river systems such as the Mississippi, Amazon, and Zambezi. Northernmost confirmed sighting in USA: Alton, Illinois.
DIET: Bony fish, rays, turtles, dolphins, crustaceans, birds, and other sharks.
DISTINGUISHING FEATURES: Stocky body, broad flat snout, small eyes, and large triangular serrated teeth; lacks a strong color contrast between upper and lower surfaces.
ANATOMY & ADAPTATIONS: Highly developed osmoregulatory system allows tolerance of both salt and fresh water. Powerful musculature and large pectoral fins enable strong bursts of speed and maneuverability. Electroreceptors detect prey in turbid water.
BEHAVIOR: Aggressive, territorial, and often solitary. Hunts by ambush in shallow water and can reach speeds of 25 mph in short bursts. Frequently travels upriver for feeding and breeding.
REPRODUCTION: Viviparous; gestation about 10–11 months; litters of 1–13 pups born in freshwater nursery zones.
PREDATORS: Large sharks, including tiger and great white sharks, and humans.
DANGER TO HUMANS: High; responsible for many nearshore attacks due to habitat overlap with swimmers.
CONSERVATION STATUS: "Vulnerable." Declining due to habitat loss, pollution, and overfishing.
NOTABLE FACTS: One of the few shark species able to survive indefinitely in freshwater. Known for exceptional adaptability and strength. Called the "Zambezi shark" in Africa and "Nicaragua shark" in Central America.

Bull shark, *Carcharhinus leucas*. Copyright © Lochlainn Seabrook.

CLADOSELACHE

COMMON NAME: Cladoselache.
SCIENTIFIC NAME: *Cladoselache fyleri* (Newberry, 1889).
FAMILY: Cladoselachidae.
GROUP: Cladoselachids.
BIOLOGICAL STATUS: Extinct.
TIME ON EARTH: About 370 million years ago.
GEOLOGIC AGE: Late Devonian Period.
SIZE: Up to 6 ft long and about 100–150 lb.
HABITAT: Warm, shallow coastal seas.
DEPTH RANGE: Surface to roughly 500 ft.
GEOGRAPHIC RANGE: Fossils found in the Cleveland Shale of Ohio and other North American Devonian deposits.
DIET: Small fish, cephalopods, and soft-bodied marine animals.
DISTINGUISHING FEATURES: Streamlined torpedo-shaped body, terminal mouth, and heterocercal tail with narrow fin lobes.
ANATOMY & ADAPTATIONS: Possessed smooth skin lacking dermal denticles, a cartilaginous skeleton, and five to seven gill slits. Its teeth were smooth-edged and suited for grasping rather than cutting. Large pectoral fins provided stability, while its crescent tail enabled sustained swimming. The absence of claspers in known specimens suggests separate male anatomy or poor preservation. Internal organ impressions reveal a two-lobed liver and advanced gill structures, rare among Devonian fossils.
BEHAVIOR: A swift, active pursuit predator capable of bursts around 25 mph. Likely hunted in open water, using vision and lateral line sensitivity to locate prey. Its agility and streamlined body allowed fast directional changes when chasing schools of early bony fishes. Possibly migrated seasonally within shallow marine corridors to follow prey concentrations.
REPRODUCTION: Probably gave live birth, inferred from internal anatomy and absence of egg cases. Embryonic structures found in related taxa support viviparity.
PREDATORS: Larger armored fishes and early placoderms.
DANGER TO HUMANS: None; long extinct.
CONSERVATION STATUS: Not applicable.
NOTABLE FACTS: Cladoselache is one of the earliest well-preserved sharks known, showing advanced hydrodynamic design long before modern species evolved. It bridges primitive and modern shark traits, marking a key stage in early elasmobranch evolution.

Cladoselache, *Cladoselache fyleri*. Copyright © Lochlainn Seabrook.

COOKIECUTTER SHARK

COMMON NAME: Cookiecutter shark.
SCIENTIFIC NAME: *Isistius brasiliensis* (Quoy and Gaimard, 1824).
FAMILY: Dalatiidae.
GROUP: Cookiecutter sharks.
BIOLOGICAL STATUS: Living.
TIME ON EARTH: About 23 million years.
GEOLOGIC AGE: Miocene to present.
SIZE: Average 16–20 in; females up to 22 in; 2–3 lb.
HABITAT: Deep pelagic waters of tropical and subtropical oceans.
DEPTH RANGE: 330 to 12,000 ft, migrates vertically toward surface at night.
GEOGRAPHIC RANGE: Circumglobal in warm waters; Atlantic, Pacific, and Indian Oceans.
DIET: Predatory and parasitic feeder; removes circular plugs of flesh from large fish, squid, whales, and even submarine cables.
DISTINGUISHING FEATURES: Cigar-shaped body, short blunt snout, large eyes, and a suctorial mouth lined with sharp triangular lower teeth that form a continuous cutting edge.
ANATOMY & ADAPTATIONS: Possesses specialized lips that form suction, allowing the shark to attach to prey before twisting to extract tissue. The lower teeth are shed and swallowed as new rows develop. Has a ventral photophore band that glows green, masking its silhouette and leaving a dark collar that lures predators and prey upward. Spins its body to carve out 2 inch holes in flesh.
BEHAVIOR: Nocturnal, solitary, and highly migratory. Ascends to near-surface waters at night to feed, returning to depths by day. Swims slowly but attacks with short, rapid bursts up to 5 mph. Known to follow ships and submarines at night, mistaking hull vibrations for prey.
REPRODUCTION: Ovoviviparous; females bear litters of 6–12 pups about 6 in long.
PREDATORS: Larger pelagic sharks and bony fish.
DANGER TO HUMANS: Minimal; rarely encountered.
CONSERVATION STATUS: "Least Concern."
NOTABLE FACTS: Leaves perfectly round holes that have identified its presence on whales and submarine equipment. Bioluminescence pattern is unique among sharks and is used in advanced camouflage research. First described in 1824, it remains one of the ocean's most unusual parasites. Sometimes caught in deep-sea nets but almost never seen alive in its natural habitat.

Cookiecutter shark, *Isistius brasiliensis*. Copyright © Lochlainn Seabrook.

EPAULETTE SHARK

COMMON NAME: Epaulette shark.
SCIENTIFIC NAME: *Hemiscyllium ocellatum* (Bonnaterre, 1788).
FAMILY: Hemiscylliidae.
GROUP: Carpet sharks.
BIOLOGICAL STATUS: Living.
TIME ON EARTH: About 20 million years.
GEOLOGIC AGE: Miocene to present.
SIZE: Average 3.3 ft; up to 4 ft; typically about 6.5 lb.
HABITAT: Shallow coral reefs, tidal pools, and sandy flats.
DEPTH RANGE: Surface to 150 ft.
GEOGRAPHIC RANGE: Northern Australia and Southern New Guinea.
DIET: Small fish, crustaceans, worms, and mollusks.
DISTINGUISHING FEATURES: Long slender body, broad rounded head, short snout, and two large black "epaulettes" (ocelli) bordered with white behind each pectoral fin.
ANATOMY & ADAPTATIONS: Possesses muscular pectoral and pelvic fins used for "walking" along the seafloor and over coral heads. Highly tolerant of low oxygen, allowing survival in isolated tidal pools during low tide. Can slow its heart rate and metabolism dramatically to endure hypoxia for up to an hour. Eyes adapted for low light in turbid shallows.
BEHAVIOR: Nocturnal and solitary. Spends daylight hours resting under coral ledges. Actively hunts at night using electroreception and olfaction. Moves by crawling or swimming in short bursts up to 2 mph. Often observed leaving water temporarily to move between tide pools.
REPRODUCTION: Oviparous; females lay pairs of small, rectangular egg cases secured to coral. Incubation lasts 110–130 days depending on temperature.
PREDATORS: Larger reef fish, sea snakes, and wading birds.
DANGER TO HUMANS: Harmless; docile and easily handled by divers.
CONSERVATION STATUS: "Least Concern."
NOTABLE FACTS: First shark documented to "walk" between reef pools using its fins. Can survive complete oxygen loss longer than any other shark. Often studied for insights into vertebrate evolution and hypoxia tolerance. Sometimes seen hunting in only inches of water during low tide. Popular in public aquariums for its small size, resilience, and unusual locomotive ability.

Epaulette shark, *Hemiscyllium ocellatum*. Copyright © Lochlainn Seabrook.

FRILLED SHARK

COMMON NAME: Frilled shark.
SCIENTIFIC NAME: *Chlamydoselachus anguineus* (Garman, 1884).
FAMILY: Chlamydoselachidae.
GROUP: Frilled sharks.
BIOLOGICAL STATUS: Living.
TIME ON EARTH: About 80 million years.
GEOLOGIC AGE: Late Cretaceous to present.
SIZE: Up to 6.5 ft long; average weight 40–70 lb, up to 250 lb.
HABITAT: Deep, cold, outer continental and upper slope waters.
DEPTH RANGE: 390–5,000 ft.
GEOGRAPHIC RANGE: Patchy global distribution in the Atlantic and Pacific Oceans, including Japan, Norway, South Africa, New Zealand, and California.
DIET: Squid, bony fish, smaller sharks, and cephalopods.
DISTINGUISHING FEATURES: Long eel-like body; broad flattened head; large terminal mouth; tricuspid teeth arranged in 25 rows; six pairs of frilled gill slits.
ANATOMY & ADAPTATIONS: Possesses primitive skeletal traits, a single dorsal fin, and terminal jaws extending forward during feeding. Its long body allows serpentine swimming. Highly distensible jaws and backward-pointing teeth prevent prey escape. Low-density liver provides buoyancy at great depth. Electroreceptors detect prey movement in darkness.
BEHAVIOR: Slow-moving ambush predator that lunges at prey with sudden bursts of speed up to 6 mph. Usually solitary, spends most of its life cruising near the seafloor or midwater. Often hunts vertically, rising from below to capture squid or fish.
REPRODUCTION: Ovoviviparous with an exceptionally long gestation period estimated at 3.5 years. Produces litters of 2–15 pups about 24 inches long.
PREDATORS: Larger deep-sea sharks and occasionally humans via bycatch.
DANGER TO HUMANS: Harmless; rarely encountered due to deep habitat.
CONSERVATION STATUS: Listed as "Least Concern" globally but vulnerable locally from deep-sea trawling.
NOTABLE FACTS: Considered a living fossil retaining many ancestral shark features. Named for the frilled appearance of its gills. Captures prey by bending its body and striking snake-like with jaws extended.

Frilled shark, *Chlamydoselachus anguineus*. Copyright © Lochlainn Seabrook.

GALAPAGOS SHARK

COMMON NAME: Galapagos shark.

SCIENTIFIC NAME: *Carcharhinus galapagensis* (Snodgrass and Heller, 1905).

FAMILY: Carcharhinidae.

GROUP: Requiem sharks.

BIOLOGICAL STATUS: Living.

TIME ON EARTH: Approximately 15 million years.

GEOLOGIC AGE: Middle Miocene to Recent.

SIZE: Commonly 9–10 ft long; up to 12 ft; average weight 190 lb.

HABITAT: Warm tropical and subtropical waters near oceanic islands.

DEPTH RANGE: Surface to about 1,800 ft; usually above 500 ft.

GEOGRAPHIC RANGE: Found worldwide near remote islands such as the Galápagos, Cocos, and Hawaiian Islands, and occasionally along continental coasts.

DIET: Bony fishes, cephalopods, rays, smaller sharks, and crustaceans.

DISTINGUISHING FEATURES: Long, slim body; rounded snout; tall first dorsal fin placed forward; gray-brown upper body with white underside; no markings.

ANATOMY & ADAPTATIONS: Streamlined body for efficiency in strong currents; powerful tail for bursts of speed; large, serrated teeth adapted for seizing prey; strong olfactory senses for detecting fish schools; well-developed eyes for moderate-light hunting.

BEHAVIOR: Highly territorial and curious; often patrols reef slopes in small groups; aggressive toward intruders and other shark species. Known to swim continuously in search of food and to exhibit dominance displays when threatened. Estimated cruising speed about 3–5 mph, with bursts near 20 mph.

REPRODUCTION: Viviparous; gestation lasts about one year; litters contain 6–16 pups about 2.5 ft long at birth.

PREDATORS: Larger sharks and orcas; juveniles vulnerable to cannibalism.

DANGER TO HUMANS: Considered potentially dangerous due to size and territorial nature; several confirmed attacks.

CONSERVATION STATUS: "Near Threatened." Populations declining from overfishing and habitat loss.

NOTABLE FACTS: The species dominates reef ecosystems around oceanic islands and is often mistaken for the dusky or gray reef shark. It plays a critical role in maintaining ecological balance.

Galapagos shark, *Carcharhinus galapagensis*. Copyright © Lochlainn Seabrook.

GANGES SHARK

COMMON NAME: Ganges shark.
SCIENTIFIC NAME: *Glyphis gangeticus* (Müller and Henle, 1839).
FAMILY: Carcharhinidae.
GROUP: River sharks.
BIOLOGICAL STATUS: Living.
TIME ON EARTH: Pleistocene to present.
GEOLOGIC AGE: Quaternary Period.
SIZE: Up to 6.5 ft, about 200 lb.
HABITAT: Turbid freshwater rivers, primarily deep channels with low visibility.
DEPTH RANGE: Surface to about 100 ft.
GEOGRAPHIC RANGE: Endemic to the Ganges, Hooghly, and Brahmaputra River systems of India and Bangladesh.
DIET: Bony fish, crustaceans, and small aquatic mammals.
DISTINGUISHING FEATURES: Broad, rounded snout; small eyes; tall first dorsal fin; short, stocky body; and narrowly triangular serrated teeth.
ANATOMY & ADAPTATIONS: Possesses highly sensitive electroreceptors suited to murky water. Reduced vision compensated by advanced ampullae of Lorenzini. Gills and kidneys adapted for low-salinity environments. Muscular body allows efficient movement in strong currents.
BEHAVIOR: Solitary and reclusive. Prefers slow swimming and ambush feeding near the riverbed. Capable of brief bursts up to 7 mph when striking prey. Often mistaken for bull sharks due to similar habitat, but it is genetically distinct.
REPRODUCTION: Viviparous, producing 6–10 pups per litter. Young are born fully developed and remain in sheltered shallows before moving into deeper channels.
PREDATORS: Large crocodiles and humans.
DANGER TO HUMANS: Extremely rare contact; generally avoids people. Unverified local accounts of attacks are likely misidentifications.
CONSERVATION STATUS: "Critically Endangered"; population severely reduced by fishing, pollution, and river damming. Protected under Indian law.
NOTABLE FACTS: One of only a few sharks living entirely in freshwater. Once common along the lower Ganges, it is now among the world's rarest sharks, with fewer than a dozen confirmed specimens in modern records.

Ganges shark, *Glyphis gangeticus*. Copyright © Lochlainn Seabrook.

GINSU SHARK

COMMON NAME: Ginsu shark.
SCIENTIFIC NAME: *Cretoxyrhina mantelli* (Agassiz, 1843).
FAMILY: Cretoxyrhinidae.
GROUP: Mackerel sharks.
BIOLOGICAL STATUS: Extinct.
TIME ON EARTH: Late Cretaceous Period.
GEOLOGIC AGE: Approximately 100–82 million years ago.
SIZE: Up to 23 ft long; estimated weight about 4 tons.
HABITAT: Warm, shallow epicontinental seas.
DEPTH RANGE: Surface to around 1,000 ft.
GEOGRAPHIC RANGE: Fossil evidence from North America, Europe, Asia, and New Zealand.
DIET: Large fish, smaller sharks, ammonites, and marine reptiles such as mosasaurs.
DISTINGUISHING FEATURES: Streamlined, torpedo-shaped body; pointed snout; large crescent tail; blade-like teeth up to 2.5 inches long.
ANATOMY & ADAPTATIONS: Powerful jaws with multiple cutting tooth rows; strong, muscular trunk for rapid pursuit; cartilaginous skeleton for buoyancy; large gill openings enabling high oxygen intake; dermal denticles reducing drag during speed bursts. Its enlarged pectoral fins provided lift and control for high-speed maneuverability.
BEHAVIOR: Fast, active predator capable of bursts near 25 mph; likely ambushed prey from below or behind; solitary hunter dominating mid-level marine food chains. Its hunting strategy favored precision strikes rather than prolonged chases.
REPRODUCTION: Viviparous, giving birth to live pups; litter size probably small, with well-developed young.
PREDATORS: Few known threats as an adult; juveniles may have been preyed upon by large mosasaurs or other sharks.
DANGER TO HUMANS: None; species extinct.
CONSERVATION STATUS: Extinct, known only from fossil remains.
NOTABLE FACTS: One of the largest lamniform sharks of the Cretaceous seas, *Cretoxyrhina* was an apex predator that predated *Carcharodon megalodon*. Its knife-edged teeth inspired the nickname "Ginsu Shark." Fossils from formations such as the Niobrara Chalk provide key evolutionary insight into modern great white ancestry, illustrating the early perfection of lamniform design.

Ginsu shark, *Cretoxyrhina mantelli*. Copyright © Lochlainn Seabrook.

GOBLIN SHARK

COMMON NAME: Goblin shark.
SCIENTIFIC NAME: *Mitsukurina owstoni* (Jordan, 1898).
FAMILY: Mitsukurinidae.
GROUP: Goblin shark.
BIOLOGICAL STATUS: Living.
TIME ON EARTH: Over 125 million years.
GEOLOGIC AGE: Early Cretaceous–Present.
SIZE: Up to 12.6 ft; average weight about 460 lb.
HABITAT: Deep-sea continental slopes and submarine canyons.
DEPTH RANGE: 330–4,300 ft, occasionally deeper.
GEOGRAPHIC RANGE: Widely scattered in the Atlantic, Pacific, and Indian Oceans, especially off Japan, South Africa, and the Gulf of America.
DIET: Teleost fish, squid, and crustaceans.
DISTINGUISHING FEATURES: Long flattened snout, highly protrusible jaws, nail-like teeth, soft pinkish body, and flabby musculature.
ANATOMY & ADAPTATIONS: Equipped with specialized jaw ligaments that allow rapid jaw projection for suction feeding. Its elongated rostrum houses numerous ampullae of Lorenzini for detecting prey electrically. Weak muscles and reduced skeleton reflect adaptation to low-energy deep-sea life. Pale skin lacks pigment, giving a translucent appearance. Highly flexible jaws can extend nearly 10 percent of total body length.
BEHAVIOR: Slow-moving ambush predator using electroreception to locate prey, then lunges forward at about 10 mph, extending its jaws to seize small fish or squid. May drift motionless to conserve energy in cold, dark waters. Believed solitary except during mating. Rarely observed alive due to extreme depth habitat.
REPRODUCTION: Ovoviviparous; embryos develop inside the mother and are born live. Litter size unknown.
PREDATORS: Large deep-water sharks. Humans pose the main threat through bycatch.
DANGER TO HUMANS: Minimal; deep habitat prevents encounters.
CONSERVATION STATUS: "Data Deficient."
NOTABLE FACTS: Sometimes called a "living fossil" due to its primitive features. The species was first described in 1898 from Japan, where it remains most frequently recorded. It is the only living representative of its family.

Goblin shark, *Mitsukurina owstoni*. Copyright © Lochlainn Seabrook.

GREAT HAMMERHEAD

COMMON NAME: Great hammerhead.

SCIENTIFIC NAME: *Sphyrna mokarran* (Rüppell, 1837).

FAMILY: Sphyrnidae.

GROUP: Hammerhead sharks.

BIOLOGICAL STATUS: Living.

TIME ON EARTH: Approximately 20 million years.

GEOLOGIC AGE: Early Miocene to present.

SIZE: Up to 20 ft; weight to 500–1,000 lb.

HABITAT: Coastal and continental shelf waters in warm and tropical seas.

DEPTH RANGE: Surface to about 900 ft.

GEOGRAPHIC RANGE: Global in tropical and subtropical regions, most common in the western Atlantic, Indian Ocean, and Indo-Pacific.

DIET: Rays, bony fish, smaller sharks, cephalopods, and crustaceans.

DISTINGUISHING FEATURES: Extremely wide, nearly straight hammer-shaped head (cephalofoil) with eyes at tips; tall, curved first dorsal fin; grayish-brown upper body and white underside.

ANATOMY & ADAPTATIONS: The broad cephalofoil provides lift, improved maneuverability, and expanded electroreception for detecting prey buried in sand. Ampullae of Lorenzini are concentrated along the head for heightened sensitivity. Long gill slits enhance oxygen intake. Large serrated teeth handle slippery or armored prey.

BEHAVIOR: Solitary and highly mobile predator known for active cruising and tight turning capability. Uses lateral sweeps of the head to locate hidden prey. Migrates seasonally following temperature shifts. Capable of bursts to about 20 mph.

REPRODUCTION: Viviparous; gestation around 11 months; litters of 6–42 pups born at roughly 2 ft in length. Maturity reached near 8 ft.

PREDATORS: Larger sharks such as tiger sharks; humans.

DANGER TO HUMANS: Potentially dangerous due to size and strength, though attacks are rare.

CONSERVATION STATUS: "Critically Endangered." Population declines from finning and bycatch.

NOTABLE FACTS: Largest of all hammerheads. Distinctive dorsal fin often mistaken for a shark of greater size. Plays key ecological role controlling ray populations.

Great hammerhead, *Sphyrna mokarran*. Copyright © Lochlainn Seabrook.

GREAT WHITE SHARK

COMMON NAME: Great white shark.

SCIENTIFIC NAME: *Carcharodon carcharias* (Linnaeus, 1758).

FAMILY: Lamnidae.

GROUP: Mackerel sharks.

BIOLOGICAL STATUS: Living.

TIME ON EARTH: Approximately 16 million years.

GEOLOGIC AGE: Middle Miocene to present.

SIZE: Typically 13–16 ft; maximum verified length 20 ft; males weigh 1,500–2,400 lb; females weigh 1,500–4,200 lb.

HABITAT: Coastal and offshore temperate and subtropical waters.

DEPTH RANGE: Surface to about 4,000 ft.

GEOGRAPHIC RANGE: Global distribution; most common off South Africa, Australia, California, and the Mediterranean.

DIET: Primarily marine mammals such as seals and sea lions; also fish, rays, and carrion.

DISTINGUISHING FEATURES: Conical snout, crescent tail, large serrated teeth, black eyes, and stark gray-white countershading.

ANATOMY & ADAPTATIONS: Streamlined, torpedo-shaped body; powerful crescent tail for bursts of speed; endothermic system allows body temperature regulation for cold-water hunting; acute vision and electroreception via ampullae of Lorenzini; rows of triangular serrated teeth for cutting flesh.

BEHAVIOR: Solitary apex predator showing curiosity and investigative biting; known to breach while hunting seals; highly migratory, traveling thousands of miles; capable of short bursts reaching about 25 mph.

REPRODUCTION: Ovoviviparous; embryos develop inside the female and are born live; litter size 2–10 pups; gestation about 12–18 months; newborns measure 4–5 ft.

PREDATORS: Orcas occasionally kill adults; juveniles vulnerable to larger sharks.

DANGER TO HUMANS: Responsible for the majority of unprovoked shark attacks; bites are investigative rather than predatory.

CONSERVATION STATUS: "Vulnerable"; population decline due to fishing, bycatch, and low reproductive rate.

NOTABLE FACTS: Only living member of its genus; teeth closely resemble those of the extinct *Carcharocles megalodon*, suggesting a distant evolutionary link. Known for breaching behavior unique among large sharks.

Great white shark, *Carcharodon carcharias*. Copyright © Lochlainn Seabrook.

GREENLAND SHARK

COMMON NAME: Greenland shark.

SCIENTIFIC NAME: *Somniosus microcephalus* (Bloch and Schneider, 1801).

FAMILY: Somniosidae.

GROUP: Sleeper sharks.

BIOLOGICAL STATUS: Living.

TIME ON EARTH: Over 100 million years.

GEOLOGIC AGE: Early Cretaceous to present.

SIZE: Commonly 21 ft; weight 880–2,200 lb.

HABITAT: Arctic and subarctic waters.

DEPTH RANGE: Surface to about 7,200 ft. Favors fjords.

GEOGRAPHIC RANGE: North Atlantic and Arctic Oceans, from eastern Canada and Greenland to Scandinavia and Russia.

DIET: Fish, squid, seals, carrion, and scavenged marine mammals.

DISTINGUISHING FEATURES: Large cylindrical body, small dorsal fins, short rounded snout, gray-brown coloration, and sluggish swimming style.

ANATOMY & ADAPTATIONS: Possesses small, asymmetric teeth; thick skin; and a slow metabolism suited to near-freezing waters. Flesh contains trimethylamine oxide and urea, making it toxic if not prepared properly. Extremely long-lived, with radiocarbon analysis showing lifespans of 250–500 years, the longest known of any vertebrate. Internal organs contain antifreeze compounds that prevent freezing damage.

BEHAVIOR: Solitary and slow-moving, averaging 0.7 mph. Uses stealth and ambush tactics rather than pursuit. Often scavenges but will actively hunt seals beneath ice. Its extremely low metabolic rate supports survival in cold, low-food environments. Can remain motionless for long periods while conserving energy.

REPRODUCTION: Ovoviviparous; females bear up to 10 pups after an estimated gestation of several years.

PREDATORS: Rarely attacked; killer whales and humans pose minimal threat.

DANGER TO HUMANS: Minimal; deep-water (deep basin) species with no verified attacks.

CONSERVATION STATUS: "Near Threatened" due to bycatch and slow reproduction.

NOTABLE FACTS: Possibly the slowest-swimming and longest-living shark. Eyes are often parasitized by copepods, reducing vision but aiding in lure-based feeding. Site fidelity.

Greenland shark, *Somniosus microcephalus*. Copyright © Lochlainn Seabrook.

HORN SHARK

COMMON NAME: Horn shark.
SCIENTIFIC NAME: *Heterodontus francisci* (Girard, 1855).
FAMILY: Heterodontidae.
GROUP: Bullhead sharks.
BIOLOGICAL STATUS: Living.
TIME ON EARTH: About 200 million years.
GEOLOGIC AGE: Early Jurassic–Recent.
SIZE: Averages 3.3 ft; up to 4 ft; weight 20–30 lb.
HABITAT: Rocky reefs, kelp forests, and sandy shallows.
DEPTH RANGE: Surface to 650 ft.
GEOGRAPHIC RANGE: Eastern Pacific, from central California to the Gulf of California.
DIET: Sea urchins, crustaceans, mollusks, small fish, and worms.
DISTINGUISHING FEATURES: Short blunt head with prominent hornlike ridges above the eyes; piglike snout; two dorsal fins each with a sharp spine; small mouth with molarlike teeth for crushing prey.
ANATOMY & ADAPTATIONS: Heavy body with tough skin and broad pectoral fins for maneuvering near the seafloor. Equipped with strong jaws and specialized dentition for grinding hard-shelled invertebrates. Uses suction and biting to extract prey from crevices. Excellent olfactory senses aid nocturnal foraging. Possesses small spiracles that allow respiration while resting motionless on the bottom.
BEHAVIOR: Solitary and slow-moving, usually sedentary during the day and active at night. Swims at about 2 mph. Known for returning repeatedly to the same resting site. Often wedges into rock crevices for protection. Uses a combination of scent and electroreception to locate buried prey.
REPRODUCTION: Oviparous. Females lay spiral-shaped egg cases, which they twist into rocky cracks for safety. Gestation lasts several months; hatchlings measure about 6 in. Matures at 10 years.
PREDATORS: Larger sharks, sea lions, and groupers.
DANGER TO HUMANS: Harmless unless provoked; dorsal spines can inflict painful wounds if handled carelessly.
CONSERVATION STATUS: "Least Concern."
NOTABLE FACTS: Known for its site fidelity, the horn shark may spend its entire life within a small coastal area. Egg cases are among the most distinctive of all sharks. Its gentle habits make it a frequent resident of public aquariums worldwide.

Horn shark, *Heterodontus francisci*. Copyright © Lochlainn Seabrook.

JAPANESE SAWSHARK

COMMON NAME: Japanese sawshark.
SCIENTIFIC NAME: *Pristiophorus japonicus* (Günther, 1870).
FAMILY: Pristiophoridae.
GROUP: Sawsharks.
BIOLOGICAL STATUS: Living.
TIME ON EARTH: About 50 million years.
GEOLOGIC AGE: Eocene to present.
SIZE: Up to 4.6 ft; weighs around 19 lb.
HABITAT: Continental shelf and upper slope.
DEPTH RANGE: 160–2,000 ft.
GEOGRAPHIC RANGE: Northwestern Pacific Ocean, including Japan, Taiwan, and parts of Korea.
DIET: Small bony fish, crustaceans, and cephalopods.
DISTINGUISHING FEATURES: Long, flattened snout lined with sharp lateral teeth; barbels positioned halfway along the rostrum; slender body; two small dorsal fins without spines; yellowish-gray dorsal surface and pale ventral side.
ANATOMY & ADAPTATIONS: The saw-like rostrum serves as both a sensory and hunting organ, detecting electrical fields and slashing through schools of prey. Small, numerous teeth allow gripping slippery fish. Barbels aid in locating food within sediment. Lightweight skeleton and reduced swim bladder enable hovering close to the seafloor. Eyes are moderately developed for low-light.
BEHAVIOR: A slow-swimming, bottom-dwelling ambush predator that uses lateral sweeps of its snout to stun or cut prey before consuming it. Usually solitary except during breeding. Speed is moderate, estimated around 3–5 mph during foraging bursts. Primarily nocturnal, moving into shallower waters at night to feed. Sometimes follows tidal movements to exploit feeding opportunities.
REPRODUCTION: Ovoviviparous, with litters of 10–20 pups. Embryos develop inside eggs retained within the mother until hatching. Newborns measure about 13–16 in. long.
PREDATORS: Larger sharks and some marine mammals.
DANGER TO HUMANS: Harmless; poses no threat.
CONSERVATION STATUS: Listed as "Least Concern," though locally affected by trawl and bycatch fisheries.
NOTABLE FACTS: The rostrum teeth regrow continuously throughout life. Its unusual appearance often causes it to be confused with sawfish, though the two are unrelated.

Japanese sawshark, *Pristiophorus japonicus*. Copyright © Lochlainn Seabrook.

KITEFIN SHARK

COMMON NAME: Kitefin shark.

SCIENTIFIC NAME: *Dalatias licha* (Bonnaterre, 1788).

FAMILY: Dalatiidae.

GROUP: Kitefin sharks.

BIOLOGICAL STATUS: Living.

TIME ON EARTH: About 60 million years.

GEOLOGIC AGE: Paleocene to present.

SIZE: 3.3–4.6 ft long; weight 18–23 lb.

HABITAT: Deep-sea continental and insular slopes.

DEPTH RANGE: 650–6,500 ft, most common below 1,300 ft.

GEOGRAPHIC RANGE: Widely distributed in temperate and tropical oceans, including the Atlantic, Pacific, and Indian Oceans, and the Mediterranean Sea.

DIET: Bony fish, squid, crustaceans, and carrion; occasionally scavenges larger prey.

DISTINGUISHING FEATURES: Stout cylindrical body, blunt snout, small dorsal fins of similar size, and lack of an anal fin. Skin covered with minute dark dermal denticles giving a velvet-like texture. Eyes large and greenish.

ANATOMY & ADAPTATIONS: Possesses dense, oily liver aiding neutral buoyancy. Slow metabolism supports life in cold, low-oxygen environments. Large jaws with sharp, triangular lower teeth used to gouge flesh from prey. Bioluminescent skin emits faint blue-green light for counterillumination camouflage in deep water. Exhibits extreme longevity typical of deep-dwelling sharks. Estimated lifespan exceeds 50 years.

BEHAVIOR: Solitary, slow-moving predator that patrols midwater and near-bottom zones at about 2–3 mph. Often follows schools of fish or feeds opportunistically on wounded or sleeping prey. Observed resting motionless on the seafloor between foraging.

REPRODUCTION: Aplacental viviparous; females give birth to 10–20 pups after a long gestation. Newborns measure around 1 ft and are fully independent.

PREDATORS: Larger sharks and deep-sea fishes.

DANGER TO HUMANS: Harmless; rarely encountered.

CONSERVATION STATUS: "Near Threatened" due to deep-sea fishing bycatch and slow reproductive rate.

NOTABLE FACTS: The largest known bioluminescent shark species. Sometimes called the "shadow shark" for its dark velvet skin and glowing underbelly.

Kitefin shark, *Dalatias licha*. Copyright © Lochlainn Seabrook.

LEMON SHARK

COMMON NAME: Lemon shark.
SCIENTIFIC NAME: *Negaprion brevirostris* (Poey, 1868).
FAMILY: Carcharhinidae.
GROUP: Requiem sharks.
BIOLOGICAL STATUS: Living.
TIME ON EARTH: ~56 million years.
GEOLOGIC AGE: Eocene to present.
SIZE: Averages 8–10 ft, up to 11 ft; weight 150–420 lb.
HABITAT: Warm, shallow coastal waters, reefs, and lagoons.
DEPTH RANGE: Surface to about 300 ft.
GEOGRAPHIC RANGE: Western Atlantic from New Jersey to southern Brazil; eastern Pacific from Baja California to Ecuador; Caribbean and Gulf of America.
DIET: Bony fish, crustaceans, rays, and small sharks.
DISTINGUISHING FEATURES: Stocky yellow-brown body, short blunt snout, small eyes, and two equal dorsal fins.
ANATOMY & ADAPTATIONS: Strong electroreception enables detection of hidden prey. Large gill area supports active swimming in warm, oxygen-rich waters. Skin color provides camouflage in sandy environments. Highly maneuverable pectoral fins aid navigation around reefs. Excellent vision and hearing assist in locating moving prey.
BEHAVIOR: Coastal and social, often forms small groups. Hunts mostly at night using ambush and quick bursts up to 12 mph. Exhibits strong site fidelity, returning to the same areas annually. Frequently rests motionless on the sea floor. Diurnal patterns may vary with tide and temperature.
REPRODUCTION: Viviparous. Gestation lasts about 12 months, producing 4–17 pups. Nursery grounds located in shallow mangrove bays for protection. Sexually matures at 10–12 years.
PREDATORS: Larger sharks, including tiger and bull sharks.
DANGER TO HUMANS: Minimal; generally non-aggressive, but will bite if provoked or cornered. Attacks are rare but dangerous.
CONSERVATION STATUS: "Near Threatened" due to overfishing and habitat degradation.
NOTABLE FACTS: Named for its yellow hue. Capable of long-distance navigation. Known for intelligence and complex social learning. Personal encounter recorded by the author during an unprovoked charge in Florida, illustrating its bold coastal behavior. Often follows divers or boats in clear tropical waters.

Lemon shark, *Negaprion brevirostris*. Copyright © Lochlainn Seabrook.

LEOPARD SHARK

SHARK PROFILE 24

COMMON NAME: Leopard shark.

SCIENTIFIC NAME: *Triakis semifasciata* (Girard, 1855).

FAMILY: Triakidae.

GROUP: Houndsharks.

BIOLOGICAL STATUS: Living.

TIME ON EARTH: About 50 million years.

GEOLOGIC AGE: Eocene to present.

SIZE: 4–5 ft in length; up to 7 ft; average weight 20–40 lb.

HABITAT: Shallow coastal waters, bays, and estuaries.

DEPTH RANGE: Surface to 300 ft.

GEOGRAPHIC RANGE: Northeastern Pacific Ocean, from Oregon to Baja California.

DIET: Crustaceans, clams, worms, small fish, and cephalopods.

DISTINGUISHING FEATURES: Slender elongated body with dark saddle-like blotches and spots; narrow snout and oval eyes.

ANATOMY & ADAPTATIONS: Possesses electroreceptive organs for locating buried prey. Small serrated teeth adapted for crushing shells. Streamlined form allows efficient maneuvering in confined coastal areas. Spiral valve intestine maximizes nutrient absorption. Skin covered in dermal denticles reduces drag during steady swimming. Strong sense of smell detects prey from long distances in turbid water.

BEHAVIOR: Slow-moving bottom feeder that forms large schools, often segregated by sex and size. Frequently enters shallow water with incoming tides. Cruises at 2–3 mph while foraging along sandy substrates. Highly tolerant of fluctuating salinity and temperature. Occasionally rests motionless on the seafloor for hours.

REPRODUCTION: Ovoviviparous; females bear 4–33 pups after a gestation period of 10–12 months. Juveniles measure about 8–10 in. at birth and mature at roughly 3–4 ft.

PREDATORS: Larger sharks, sea lions, and occasionally humans.

DANGER TO HUMANS: Harmless; timid disposition and small teeth make bites extremely rare.

CONSERVATION STATUS: "Least Concern." Populations stable but are affected by habitat loss and pollution in estuaries.

NOTABLE FACTS: California's most commonly encountered shark; protected from commercial harvest in many coastal areas. Known for its distinctive leopard-like pattern, making it a favorite among divers and marine photographers. Often seen swimming in mixed schools with smoothhounds and bat rays.

Leopard shark, *Triakis semifasciata*. Copyright © Lochlainn Seabrook.

LONGFIN MAKO

COMMON NAME: Longfin mako.

SCIENTIFIC NAME: *Isurus paucus* (Guitart Manday, 1966).

FAMILY: Lamnidae.

GROUP: Mackerel sharks.

BIOLOGICAL STATUS: Living.

TIME ON EARTH: ~20 million years.

GEOLOGIC AGE: Early Miocene–Recent.

SIZE: Up to 14 ft in length; weight 150–450 lb.

HABITAT: Open ocean, epipelagic and mesopelagic zones.

DEPTH RANGE: Surface to 2,300 ft.

GEOGRAPHIC RANGE: Warm and temperate waters worldwide, chiefly in the Atlantic, Pacific, and Indian Oceans.

DIET: Bony fish, squid, cephalopods, and small sharks.

DISTINGUISHING FEATURES: Extremely long, narrow pectoral fins; conical snout; large black eyes; slender fusiform body; metallic blue dorsal surface and white underside.

ANATOMY & ADAPTATIONS: Streamlined form for sustained cruising; powerful lunate tail; endothermic capability via countercurrent heat exchangers allowing elevated body temperature; large gill surface for efficient oxygen uptake; long fins enhance lift and stability during slow swimming.

BEHAVIOR: Solitary, wide-ranging pelagic predator that moves through tropical and subtropical waters at cruising speeds around 5 mph, capable of bursts exceeding 20 mph. Exhibits slow, steady movements punctuated by rapid lunges when pursuing prey. Often follows thermal fronts and deep scattering layers during diel migrations, showing preference for waters above 68°F.

REPRODUCTION: Ovoviviparous; embryos develop in utero and are nourished by yolk sacs. Litters of 2–8 pups born at ~3 ft length after 15–18-month gestation.

PREDATORS: Larger sharks such as great whites and tiger sharks; orcas occasionally.

DANGER TO HUMANS: Minimal; rarely encountered due to offshore habits.

CONSERVATION STATUS: "Vulnerable." Population is declining due to bycatch and fin trade.

NOTABLE FACTS: One of the least studied lamnids. Its long fins distinguish it from the shortfin mako; both share endothermic physiology and strong migratory tendencies. Its rarity and deep-ranging habits make live observations exceptionally rare.

Longfin mako, *Isurus paucus*. Copyright © Lochlainn Seabrook.

MEGALODON

COMMON NAME: Megalodon.

SCIENTIFIC NAME: *Otodus megalodon* (Agassiz, 1843).

FAMILY: Otodontidae.

GROUP: Mackerel sharks.

BIOLOGICAL STATUS: Extinct.

TIME ON EARTH: Approximately 15 million years.

GEOLOGIC AGE: Late Miocene to Pliocene.

SIZE: Most adults averaged 45–55 ft long and weighed about 100,000 lb, though some individuals may have reached 79 ft and 240,000 lb based on current evidence.

HABITAT: Warm to temperate marine waters, including continental shelves and open-ocean margins.

DEPTH RANGE: From nearshore zones to several hundred feet deep.

GEOGRAPHIC RANGE: Global; fossil remains found in every major ocean basin.

DIET: Large marine mammals such as early whales, seals, and dolphins, along with sharks and large bony fish.

DISTINGUISHING FEATURES: Massive triangular serrated teeth up to 7 inches high; enormous jaws capable of extreme bite force; broad, torpedo-shaped body.

ANATOMY & ADAPTATIONS: Cartilaginous skeleton; mesothermic metabolism allowing extended range into cooler waters; efficient predatory design with strong jaws, thick musculature, and large pectoral fins for speed bursts.

BEHAVIOR: Dominant solitary hunter that cruised at 1.5–2 mph, capable of rapid acceleration during ambush strikes; prey likely attacked from below or behind.

REPRODUCTION: Ovoviviparous; embryos nourished through oophagy; newborns estimated at 12–13 ft in length.

PREDATORS: None known; apex predator of its era.

DANGER TO HUMANS: None—species extinct long before humans evolved (though unconfirmed modern sightings do occur).

CONSERVATION STATUS: Extinct.

NOTABLE FACTS: Both the largest predatory shark and the largest macropredatory fish known to science; extinction roughly 2.6 million years ago may have resulted from oceanic cooling and prey decline. Estimated bite force exceeded 40,000 lb per square inch. Megalodon's dominance shaped marine food chains for millions of years and inspired modern great white mythology.

Megalodon, *Otodus megalodon*. Copyright © Lochlainn Seabrook.

MEGAMOUTH SHARK

COMMON NAME: Megamouth shark.

SCIENTIFIC NAME: *Megachasma pelagios* (Taylor, Compagno, and Struhsaker, 1983).

FAMILY: Megachasmidae.

GROUP: Megamouth shark.

BIOLOGICAL STATUS: Living.

TIME ON EARTH: About 36 million years.

GEOLOGIC AGE: Late Eocene to present.

SIZE: Up to 18 ft long; weight 1,650 to 2,700 lb.

HABITAT: Deep pelagic zones near continental slopes and seamounts.

DEPTH RANGE: From surface to over 5,000 ft.

GEOGRAPHIC RANGE: Tropical and temperate waters worldwide, including the Pacific, Indian, and Atlantic Oceans.

DIET: Plankton, krill, and small jellyfish filtered through gill rakers; one of only three known filter-feeding shark species.

DISTINGUISHING FEATURES: Enormous, rounded head with a broad mouth lined by small teeth; rubbery gray-brown skin; luminous tissue inside mouth for attracting prey.

ANATOMY & ADAPTATIONS: Possesses long gill rakers for plankton feeding, soft cartilaginous structure for slow cruising, and a large liver for buoyancy. Its jaw muscles and flexible skeleton allow wide-mouth filter feeding.

BEHAVIOR: A slow, passive swimmer, rarely exceeding 2 mph. Believed to feed vertically or by slow forward motion through dense plankton clouds. Often migrates vertically following diel light and food patterns.

REPRODUCTION: Ovoviviparous, with embryos developing in egg cases inside the mother. Litter size and gestation period remain unknown due to rarity.

PREDATORS: Likely attacked by larger sharks, such as great whites and tiger sharks.

DANGER TO HUMANS: Harmless and non-aggressive. Encounters are extremely rare.

CONSERVATION STATUS: Listed as "Least Concern" by the IUCN but vulnerable to bycatch and deepwater drift nets.

NOTABLE FACTS: First described in 1976 off Oahu, Hawaii. Fewer than 300 confirmed specimens have been recorded worldwide. Its slow, reclusive, and mysterious nature makes it one of the ocean's least observed and least understood giants.

Megamouth shark, *Megachasma pelagios*. Copyright © Lochlainn Seabrook.

NURSE SHARK

COMMON NAME: Nurse shark.

SCIENTIFIC NAME: *Ginglymostoma cirratum* (Bonnaterre, 1788).

FAMILY: Ginglymostomatidae.

GROUP: Nurse sharks.

BIOLOGICAL STATUS: Living.

TIME ON EARTH: About 30 million years.

GEOLOGIC AGE: Oligocene to present.

SIZE: Typically 7.5–10 ft, up to 14 ft; 165–325 lb.

HABITAT: Warm, shallow coastal waters, coral reefs, and sandy flats.

DEPTH RANGE: From surface to 250 ft.

GEOGRAPHIC RANGE: Western and eastern Atlantic, Caribbean Sea, Gulf of America, and eastern Pacific from Baja California to Peru.

DIET: Fish, crustaceans, mollusks, and stingrays.

DISTINGUISHING FEATURES: Broad, flat head; small eyes; two dorsal fins of equal size; short barbels near nostrils; long tail without a lower lobe.

ANATOMY & ADAPTATIONS: Possesses thick, tough skin and strong suction-feeding jaws lined with small serrated teeth for crushing shells. Spiracles behind eyes aid respiration while resting on the seafloor. Uses barbels to detect buried prey. Equipped with a flexible body and broad pectoral fins for maneuvering along the bottom.

BEHAVIOR: Slow, docile, and primarily nocturnal. Hunts at night using suction to extract prey from crevices. Often rests motionless in groups during the day. Capable of short bursts up to 2 mph when startled. Occasionally congregates in large numbers under reef ledges or mangrove roots.

REPRODUCTION: Ovoviviparous; females bear 20–30 pups after a 5–6 month gestation.

PREDATORS: Larger sharks, including tiger and bull sharks.

DANGER TO HUMANS: Generally harmless but may bite defensively if provoked or stepped on.

CONSERVATION STATUS: "Near Threatened" due to overfishing and habitat degradation.

NOTABLE FACTS: One of the few sharks that can pump water over its gills while stationary, allowing long periods of rest on the seabed. Known to return to bask in the same locations for years, showing strong site fidelity.

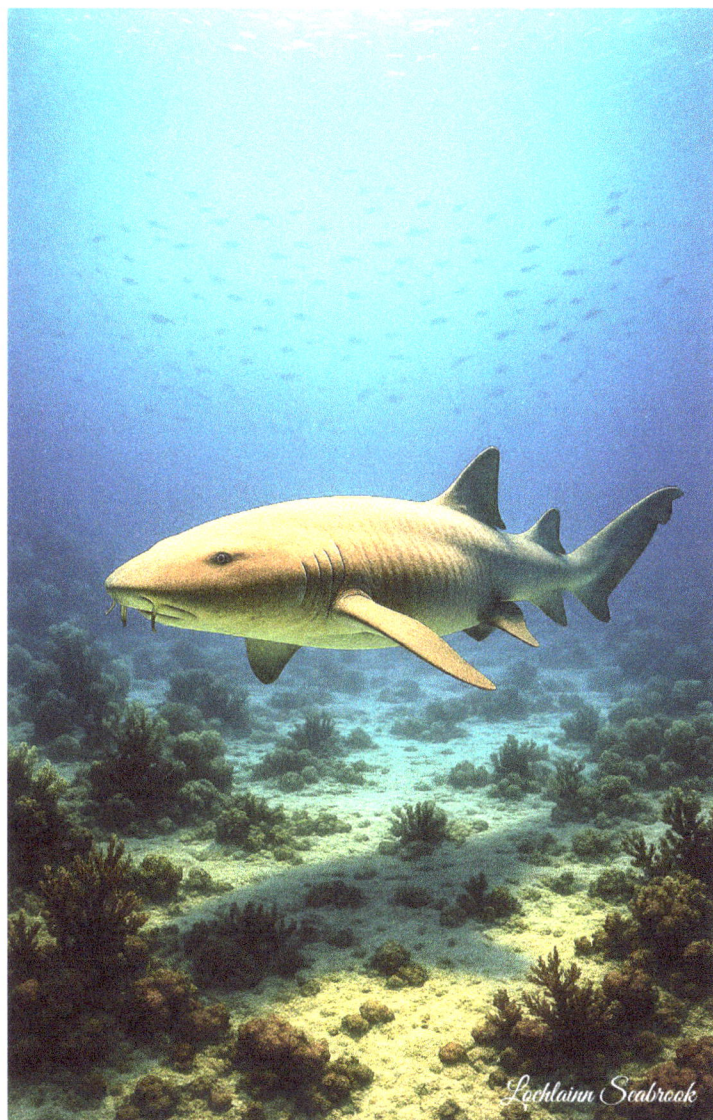

Nurse shark, *Ginglymostoma cirratum*. Copyright © Lochlainn Seabrook.

OCEANIC WHITETIP SHARK

COMMON NAME: Oceanic whitetip shark.
SCIENTIFIC NAME: *Carcharhinus longimanus* (Poey, 1861).
FAMILY: Carcharhinidae.
GROUP: Requiem sharks.
BIOLOGICAL STATUS: Living.
TIME ON EARTH: ~6 million years.
GEOLOGIC AGE: Late Miocene–Holocene.
SIZE: Up to 13 ft; 80–370 lb.
HABITAT: Open ocean, pelagic waters.
DEPTH RANGE: Surface to 500 ft.
GEOGRAPHIC RANGE: Tropical and subtropical seas worldwide between 30°N and 35°S.
DIET: Bony fish, cephalopods, seabirds, and carrion.
DISTINGUISHING FEATURES: Broad, rounded pectoral fins with white tips; stocky body; large dorsal fin; short, blunt snout.
ANATOMY & ADAPTATIONS: Possesses large pectoral fins that provide lift for slow cruising in open water; countershaded coloration aids camouflage from both prey and predators; highly developed ampullae of Lorenzini detect weak electrical signals.
BEHAVIOR: Solitary but often gathers where food is abundant; known to follow ships and pods of whales; capable of bursts up to 15 mph; aggressive and inquisitive when feeding; shows strong site fidelity and often patrols the same oceanic zones for years.
REPRODUCTION: Viviparous; gestation about 12 months; litters range from 1–15 pups, each about 2 ft long at birth; pups remain in shallow nursery areas before moving offshore.
PREDATORS: Larger sharks, particularly tiger and great white sharks; occasionally orcas.
DANGER TO HUMANS: Considered potentially dangerous; responsible for several attacks, mainly on shipwreck or plane-crash survivors; known to approach divers with bold curiosity.
CONSERVATION STATUS: "Critically Endangered" due to bycatch in longline fisheries and demand for fins; slow reproductive rate hinders population recovery; international protections have increased but enforcement remains weak.
NOTABLE FACTS: Once among the most abundant oceanic sharks; populations have declined by over 90% in some regions. Often followed WWII survivors in open seas, earning a fearful reputation. Plays an essential role in pelagic food webs, controlling mid-level predators and maintaining species balance. Now rarely encountered in waters where it was once common.

Oceanic whitetip shark, *Carcharhinus longimanus*. Copyright © Lochlainn Seabrook.

ORNATE WOBBEGONG

COMMON NAME: Ornate wobbegong.
SCIENTIFIC NAME: *Orectolobus ornatus* (De Vis, 1883).
FAMILY: Orectolobidae.
GROUP: Wobbegongs.
BIOLOGICAL STATUS: Living.
TIME ON EARTH: About 11 million years.
GEOLOGIC AGE: Late Miocene–Recent.
SIZE: 4–5 ft; rare up to 10 ft long; may average 10–30 lb.
HABITAT: Tropical and subtropical coastal waters, typically on rocky or coral reefs.
DEPTH RANGE: From the intertidal zone to about 330 ft.
GEOGRAPHIC RANGE: Western Pacific Ocean, mainly eastern Australia and southern New Guinea.
DIET: Bony fish, crustaceans, cephalopods, and occasionally smaller sharks.
DISTINGUISHING FEATURES: Broad, flattened body with elaborate dermal lobes around the mouth; irregular dark brown, yellow, and white reticulated pattern for camouflage; large head with small eyes and beard-like barbels.
ANATOMY & ADAPTATIONS: Cryptic coloration and skin flaps blend perfectly with reef surfaces. Strong jaws armed with long, sharp teeth for gripping struggling prey. Spiracles behind the eyes allow respiration while motionless on the bottom. Folds of skin along the mouth act as lures. Muscular body enables sudden ambush strikes. Dentition designed to pierce and hold slippery fish. Possesses flexible joints for quick angular strikes. Can rotate its head sharply to capture prey approaching from behind.
BEHAVIOR: Primarily nocturnal and sedentary. Lies motionless during the day, using camouflage to ambush prey. Slow swimmer but capable of quick lunges when feeding. Usually solitary and shows high site fidelity. Estimated speed 2–3 mph when cruising.
REPRODUCTION: Ovoviviparous. Embryos develop in utero and are born live; litters of up to 20 pups measuring about 8–10 in.
PREDATORS: Larger sharks and humans.
DANGER TO HUMANS: Low, though provoked individuals can inflict serious bites with powerful jaws.
CONSERVATION STATUS: "Least Concern."
NOTABLE FACTS: Name derives from Malay "wobbegong," meaning shaggy beard. Sometimes mistaken for reef growth until it moves. Excellent example of reef camouflage.

Ornate wobbegong, *Orectolobus ornatus*. Copyright © Lochlainn Seabrook.

PORBEAGLE

COMMON NAME: Porbeagle.

SCIENTIFIC NAME: *Lamna nasus* (Bonnaterre, 1788).

FAMILY: Lamnidae.

GROUP: Mackerel sharks.

BIOLOGICAL STATUS: Living.

TIME ON EARTH: At least 60 million years.

GEOLOGIC AGE: Paleocene to present.

SIZE: Commonly 7.5–9 ft; up to 12 ft; 300 lb average, maximum near 600 lb.

HABITAT: Temperate to cold offshore waters, coastal shelves, and banks.

DEPTH RANGE: Surface to 2,000 ft.

GEOGRAPHIC RANGE: North Atlantic, southern Atlantic, southern Indian, and South Pacific Oceans.

DIET: Primarily bony fishes, cephalopods, and small sharks.

DISTINGUISHING FEATURES: Streamlined, spindle-shaped body; strong crescent tail; pointed snout; white patch at base of dorsal fin.

ANATOMY & ADAPTATIONS: Possesses countercurrent heat-exchange system enabling regional endothermy; large gill surface for efficient oxygen uptake; muscular caudal peduncle for powerful swimming; large eyes for vision in dim light.

BEHAVIOR: Active, wide-ranging swimmer often near the thermocline; migrates seasonally following prey movements; capable of sustained cruising at 20 mph with bursts up to 35 mph; displays site fidelity to productive feeding grounds; sometimes hunts cooperatively in loose groups.

REPRODUCTION: Ovoviviparous; internal fertilization; litters of 1–5 well-developed pups; long gestation up to 9 months; slow reproductive rate.

PREDATORS: Larger sharks such as great whites and killer whales occasionally prey on juveniles.

DANGER TO HUMANS: Rarely aggressive; few verified attacks, usually only hostile when provoked.

CONSERVATION STATUS: "Vulnerable" globally due to overfishing and bycatch; slow growth and low fecundity hinder recovery.

NOTABLE FACTS: One of the fastest cold-water sharks; sometimes mistaken for a small great white; favored by anglers for strength; body temperature can exceed surrounding water by 10°F.

Porbeagle, *Lamna nasus*. Copyright © Lochlainn Seabrook.

SANDBAR SHARK

COMMON NAME: Sandbar shark.
SCIENTIFIC NAME: *Carcharhinus plumbeus* (Nardo, 1827).
FAMILY: Carcharhinidae.
GROUP: Requiem sharks.
BIOLOGICAL STATUS: Living.
TIME ON EARTH: Approximately 60 million years.
GEOLOGIC AGE: Paleogene to present.
SIZE: Average 6.5 ft; up to 8.2 ft; 100–200 lb.
HABITAT: Coastal/offshore waters over sandy or muddy bottoms.
DEPTH RANGE: 60–650 ft.
GEOGRAPHIC RANGE: Tropical and warm-temperate waters worldwide, including the western Atlantic, Gulf of America, Caribbean, Mediterranean, and Indo-Pacific.
DIET: Bony fishes, small sharks, rays, squid, octopus, and crustaceans.
DISTINGUISHING FEATURES: Tall, triangular first dorsal fin; short, rounded snout; broad body; gray-brown dorsum with lighter underside.
ANATOMY & ADAPTATIONS: Possesses heavy musculature and a high forward dorsal fin for stability in shallow currents. Electroreceptors detect prey beneath sediment. Broad pectoral fins provide lift, reducing energy expenditure during cruising.
BEHAVIOR: Slow, methodical swimmer, typically 3–5 mph; often travels in loose groups by size and sex. Prefers sandy shallows and estuaries, but migrates seasonally to deeper waters. Mostly nocturnal feeder.
REPRODUCTION: Viviparous. Gestation lasts about 12 months. Produces 6–14 pups about 2 ft long. Nursery areas located in warm, shallow bays.
PREDATORS: Larger sharks such as tiger and great hammerhead sharks. Juveniles vulnerable to groupers and rays.
DANGER TO HUMANS: Considered timid and rarely aggressive. Few verified attacks.
CONSERVATION STATUS: "Vulnerable" due to overfishing and slow reproductive rate.
NOTABLE FACTS: Known for its tall dorsal fin, the sandbar shark is one of the most common large coastal sharks in the western Atlantic and a key indicator species for marine ecosystem health. Its distinctive high fin often leads to confusion with other large requiem sharks by divers and fishermen.

Sandbar shark, *Carcharhinus plumbeus*. Copyright © Lochlainn Seabrook.

SAND TIGER SHARK

COMMON NAME: Sand tiger shark.
SCIENTIFIC NAME: *Carcharias taurus* (Rafinesque, 1810).
FAMILY: Odontaspididae.
GROUP: Sand tiger sharks.
BIOLOGICAL STATUS: Living.
TIME ON EARTH: About 100 million years.
GEOLOGIC AGE: Late Cretaceous to present.
SIZE: Up to 10.5 ft, 200–400 lb.
HABITAT: Coastal continental shelves, sandy shorelines, coral and rocky reefs, shallow bays, and estuaries.
DEPTH RANGE: Surface to 650 ft.
GEOGRAPHIC RANGE: Temperate and subtropical waters of the Atlantic, Pacific, and Indian Oceans, including the eastern and western U.S. coasts, Mediterranean Sea, South Africa, Japan, and Australia.
DIET: Bony fish, smaller sharks, rays, squid, and crustaceans.
DISTINGUISHING FEATURES: Broad flattened snout, small eyes, long narrow teeth visible even when the mouth is closed, and two nearly equal dorsal fins set far back on the body.
ANATOMY & ADAPTATIONS: Streamlined body with light brown to gray coloration and dark reddish spots along the sides for camouflage. Possesses an air-gulping behavior that allows it to maintain neutral buoyancy. Thick skin and robust jaw musculature for grasping slippery fish.
BEHAVIOR: Nocturnal, slow-moving predator that cruises near the seafloor. Often gathers in groups near reefs and wrecks. Capable of short bursts reaching about 6 mph when striking prey. Tolerates close proximity to divers.
REPRODUCTION: Ovoviviparous with intrauterine cannibalism; only one embryo survives per uterus after consuming its siblings. Gestation about 9–12 months.
PREDATORS: Larger sharks such as the tiger and great white, and humans through fishing.
DANGER TO HUMANS: Generally docile; provoked attacks are extremely rare.
CONSERVATION STATUS: "Vulnerable" globally due to low reproductive rate and overfishing.
NOTABLE FACTS: Despite its fierce appearance, the sand tiger shark is gentle and socially cooperative, often forming resting groups in caves or near wrecks.

Sand tiger shark, *Carcharias taurus*. Copyright © Lochlainn Seabrook.

SCALLOPED HAMMERHEAD

COMMON NAME: Scalloped hammerhead.

SCIENTIFIC NAME: *Sphyrna lewini* (Griffith and Smith, 1834).

FAMILY: Sphyrnidae.

GROUP: Hammerhead sharks.

BIOLOGICAL STATUS: Living.

TIME ON EARTH: About 20 million years.

GEOLOGIC AGE: Early Miocene to present.

SIZE: Average 10–14 ft; average male 64 lb., female 180 lb.

HABITAT: Coastal and pelagic tropical and warm-temperate seas near shelves, seamounts, and islands.

DEPTH RANGE: Surface to about 1,600 ft.

GEOGRAPHIC RANGE: Circumtropical; Atlantic, Pacific, and Indian Oceans; common near Hawaii, the Caribbean, and eastern Pacific.

DIET: Bony fishes, cephalopods, rays, and small sharks.

DISTINGUISHING FEATURES: Narrow, arched hammer-shaped head with three central scallops; tall sickle-shaped first dorsal fin; bronze-gray dorsum with pale belly.

ANATOMY & ADAPTATIONS: Broad cephalofoil improves lift, stability, and turning. Expanded sensory pores detect weak electrical fields. Lateral eyes provide wide binocular vision. Nictitating membranes protect eyes during prey capture. Gill openings long and well spaced for efficient respiration. Internal fertilization through paired claspers in males.

BEHAVIOR: Highly social, forming large daytime schools that disperse at dusk. Active swimmer reaching 20 mph. Performs vertical migrations following prey and temperature gradients. Uses electroreception to locate hidden rays and fish on sandy bottoms. Occasionally observed performing gentle rolling turns when patrolling reefs.

REPRODUCTION: Viviparous. Gestation about 12 months. Litters of 12–41 pups born at 18–20 in. Nursery areas found in shallow coastal bays.

PREDATORS: Larger sharks, especially tigers and great hammerheads.

DANGER TO HUMANS: Normally shy; few confirmed attacks.

CONSERVATION STATUS: "Critically Endangered" due to fin trade and bycatch.

NOTABLE FACTS: Named for its scalloped cephalofoil margin. First hammerhead described scientifically. Noted for mass schooling near island drop-offs. Often seen day-cruising above coral slopes.

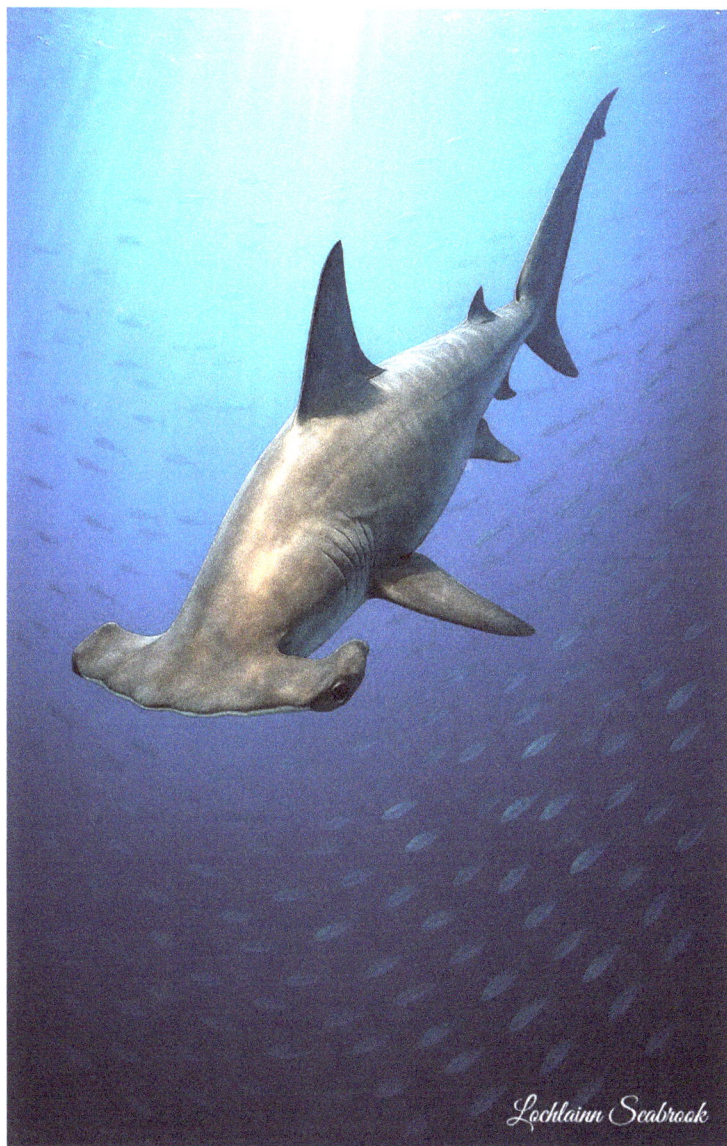

Scalloped hammerhead, *Sphyrna lewini*. Copyright © Lochlainn Seabrook.

SCISSOR-TOOTH SHARK

COMMON NAME: Scissor-tooth shark.

SCIENTIFIC NAME: *Edestus giganteus* (Leidy, 1856).

FAMILY: Edestidae.

GROUP: Eugeneodonts.

BIOLOGICAL STATUS: Extinct.

TIME ON EARTH: Approximately 315–300 million years ago.

GEOLOGIC AGE: Late Carboniferous (Pennsylvanian).

SIZE: Estimated length 20–25 ft; estimated weight 2,000–4,000 lb.

HABITAT: Offshore marine environments of ancient epicontinental seas.

DEPTH RANGE: Believed to inhabit midwater to near-surface zones up to 1,000 ft deep.

GEOGRAPHIC RANGE: Fossils found in North America, Europe, and Russia.

DIET: Likely large fish and soft-bodied marine animals.

DISTINGUISHING FEATURES: Possessed unique "scissor-like" tooth whorls in both jaws, forming a curved row of forward-projecting serrated teeth that sliced vertically through prey.

ANATOMY & ADAPTATIONS: Streamlined body with a stiff heterocercal tail suited for fast cruising. Jaws equipped with continuously growing teeth arranged in opposing curved blades that acted as shears rather than replacement rows. Lacked true biting capability; instead, fed by slicing prey apart with rapid jaw motion.

BEHAVIOR: Active predatory swimmer adapted for open-sea hunting. Likely attacked by slashing upward and downward with its tooth blades. Estimated speed 15–20 mph. Possibly pursued wounded prey until incapacitated.

REPRODUCTION: Unknown; possibly ovoviviparous like modern sharks. No egg cases known.

PREDATORS: Larger Paleozoic sharks may have preyed on juveniles.

DANGER TO HUMANS: None; extinct long before humans appeared.

CONSERVATION STATUS: Not applicable.

NOTABLE FACTS: One of the strangest sharks ever discovered. Tooth whorls grew continuously through life, pushing older teeth outward. First described scientifically in 1886 from Illinois fossils. Related to *Helicoprion* but distinguished by its vertical tooth arrangement and scissorlike feeding motion.

Scissor-tooth shark, *Edestus giganteus*. Copyright © Lochlainn Seabrook.

SHARPNOSE SEVENGILL SHARK

COMMON NAME: Sharpnose sevengill shark.
SCIENTIFIC NAME: *Heptranchias perlo* (Bonnaterre, 1788).
FAMILY: Heptranchidae.
GROUP: Cow sharks.
BIOLOGICAL STATUS: Living.
TIME ON EARTH: Approximately 150 million years.
GEOLOGIC AGE: Late Jurassic to present.
SIZE: Average 4.6 ft; maximum about 5.6 ft; 6–21 lb.
HABITAT: Continental and insular slopes, outer shelves, and upper bathyal zones.
DEPTH RANGE: 330–3,000 ft, most common below 650 ft.
GEOGRAPHIC RANGE: Widespread in tropical and temperate seas of the Atlantic, Pacific, and Indian Oceans.
DIET: Small bony fishes, cephalopods, crustaceans, and carrion.
DISTINGUISHING FEATURES: Slender body, long pointed snout, seven gill slits, single dorsal fin set far back, and greenish-gray upper coloration fading to pale underside.
ANATOMY & ADAPTATIONS: Possesses a flexible skeleton, large eyes adapted for low light, and serrated lower teeth for cutting prey. The seven gill slits improve respiration efficiency at greater depths. Its lateral line detects minute vibrations, aiding in nocturnal hunting. The elongated snout houses electroreceptors used to locate buried prey.
BEHAVIOR: A solitary, slow-cruising nocturnal predator. Prefers benthic zones and occasionally ascends to midwater at night. Capable of short bursts around 10 mph when attacking prey. Often scavenges along seafloor slopes and submarine canyons. Shows distinct avoidance of artificial light and human noise intrusion.
REPRODUCTION: Ovoviviparous; females bear litters of 9–20 pups about 10 in long. No parental care observed. Gestation period remains poorly documented but likely exceeds one year.
PREDATORS: Larger sharks such as bluntnose sixgills and bigeye threshers.
DANGER TO HUMANS: Harmless; rarely encountered due to deep habitat.
CONSERVATION STATUS: Listed as "Least Concern" globally though locally vulnerable to deep-sea trawling.
NOTABLE FACTS: The only living member of its genus. Represents one of the most primitive modern sharks, retaining ancient traits linking today's species with Jurassic ancestors. Fossil remains show minimal evolutionary change across millions of years.

Sharpnose sevengill shark, *Heptranchias perlo*. Copyright © Lochlainn Seabrook.

SHORTFIN MAKO

COMMON NAME: Shortfin mako.
SCIENTIFIC NAME: *Isurus oxyrinchus* (Rafinesque, 1810).
FAMILY: Lamnidae.
GROUP: Mackerel sharks.
BIOLOGICAL STATUS: Living.
TIME ON EARTH: About 20 million years.
GEOLOGIC AGE: Early Miocene–Present.
SIZE: Up to 13 ft long; average 135–300 lb; up to 1,300 lb.
HABITAT: Epipelagic and coastal offshore waters.
DEPTH RANGE: Surface to about 500 ft.
GEOGRAPHIC RANGE: Worldwide temperate and tropical seas.
DIET: Predatory; feeds mainly on bony fishes such as mackerel, tuna, swordfish, and squid.
DISTINGUISHING FEATURES: Streamlined torpedo body, pointed snout, large black eyes, crescent tail, and vivid metallic-blue dorsal coloration with a white underside.
ANATOMY & ADAPTATIONS: Warm-blooded lamnid with regional endothermy allowing sustained high-speed swimming. Strong lunate tail provides thrust. Long gill slits and stiff pectoral fins enhance hydrodynamics. Large conical teeth lack serrations, optimized for grasping slippery prey. Highly resistant to diseases.
BEHAVIOR: Among the fastest sharks, capable of bursts exceeding 46 mph. Highly active, solitary, and migratory. When hunting or hooked it often breaches the surface in magnificent leaping displays. Uses rapid lunging strikes from below to impale prey.
REPRODUCTION: Aplacental viviparous; embryos develop in utero and feed on unfertilized eggs. Litter size averages 4–25 pups measuring about 2 ft at birth.
PREDATORS: Large sharks and killer whales occasionally prey on juveniles. Adults have few natural enemies.
DANGER TO HUMANS: Considered potentially dangerous due to its speed, power, weight, and size, but responsible for few attacks. Encounters are rare.
CONSERVATION STATUS: "Endangered"; heavily fished for meat, fins, and sport. Populations declining worldwide from overexploitation.
NOTABLE FACTS: The shortfin mako is the fastest shark known. Its muscles generate internal heat that boosts swimming efficiency. Prized by anglers for its strength and acrobatics, it is a key species for pelagic shark research, conservation, and medical studies.

Shortfin mako, *Isurus oxyrinchus*. Copyright © Lochlainn Seabrook.

SILKY SHARK

COMMON NAME: Silky shark.
SCIENTIFIC NAME: *Carcharhinus falciformis* (Müller and Henle, 1839).
FAMILY: Carcharhinidae.
GROUP: Requiem sharks.
BIOLOGICAL STATUS: Living.
TIME ON EARTH: About 23 million years.
GEOLOGIC AGE: Miocene to present.
SIZE: Average just over 8 ft; maximum 11 ft; 392–760 lb.
HABITAT: Warm, deep pelagic waters near continental and island slopes; occasionally coastal.
DEPTH RANGE: Surface to about 1,640 ft, most common above 650 ft.
GEOGRAPHIC RANGE: Tropical and subtropical oceans worldwide between roughly 40°N and 40°S.
DIET: Small schooling fish such as tuna, mackerel, sardines, and jacks; also squid and octopus.
DISTINGUISHING FEATURES: Slender streamlined body, long sickle-shaped pectoral fins, small dorsal fin set far back, bronze-gray upper body, white underside, large eyes, pointed snout.
ANATOMY & ADAPTATIONS: Smooth dermal denticles minimize drag; large caudal fin and strong musculature provide sustained speed; high red-muscle ratio supports endurance; acute electroreception and vision aid open-ocean hunting.
BEHAVIOR: Active, fast, and social; forms large migratory schools often with tuna; cruises continuously and can reach speeds near 20 mph; shows dominance postures while feeding.
REPRODUCTION: Viviparous; gestation about 12 months; litters 2–16 pups about 2 ft long; breeding year-round in warm regions.
PREDATORS: Larger sharks including tiger and great hammerhead; orcas; juveniles vulnerable to pelagic predators.
DANGER TO HUMANS: Generally avoids people; few verified attacks, mostly provoked or bait-related.
CONSERVATION STATUS: "Vulnerable" from overfishing and fin trade bycatch; global populations declining.
NOTABLE FACTS: Named for its silky-smooth skin; among the most abundant open-ocean sharks yet heavily exploited; frequently accompanies tuna schools. Juveniles aggregate near floating debris for protection; individuals may migrate thousands of miles.

Silky shark, *Carcharhinus falciformis*. Copyright © Lochlainn Seabrook.

SMALL-SPOTTED CATSHARK

COMMON NAME: Small-spotted catshark.

SCIENTIFIC NAME: *Scyliorhinus canicula* (Linnaeus, 1758).

FAMILY: Scyliorhinidae.

GROUP: Catsharks.

BIOLOGICAL STATUS: Living.

TIME ON EARTH: Approximately 50 million years.

GEOLOGIC AGE: Eocene to present.

SIZE: Up to 3 ft long; weight 2–4.5 lb.

HABITAT: Continental shelf and upper slope regions over sandy, gravelly, or muddy bottoms.

DEPTH RANGE: Typically 30–1,300 ft.

GEOGRAPHIC RANGE: Eastern Atlantic from Norway to Senegal, including the Mediterranean and western Black Sea.

DIET: Small bony fish, crustaceans, mollusks, and worms.

DISTINGUISHING FEATURES: Slender body, elongated snout, large oval eyes with vertical pupils, two small dorsal fins far back on the body, and numerous small dark spots on a pale background.

ANATOMY & ADAPTATIONS: Possesses dermal denticles that reduce drag; sensitive lateral line detects low-frequency vibrations; eyes adapted for low light; spiracles above the eyes allow breathing while resting on the seafloor.

BEHAVIOR: Nocturnal bottom-dweller; rests motionless by day, hunts at night. Swims slowly at roughly 2–3 mph using undulating body motions close to the substrate. Capable of remaining hidden in sand or among rocks for long periods. Often found in loose groups, especially during feeding.

REPRODUCTION: Oviparous. Females lay rectangular, horned egg cases, often called "mermaid's purses," attaching them to seaweed or substrates. Embryos develop for 5–11 months depending on temperature. Juveniles hatch at about 4–5 inches long and grow slowly to maturity.

PREDATORS: Larger sharks, seals, and some bony fish.

DANGER TO HUMANS: Harmless; poses no threat.

CONSERVATION STATUS: Listed as "Least Concern" by the IUCN due to broad distribution and stable population, though localized declines occur from trawl bycatch. Managed in some regions under European fisheries regulations.

NOTABLE FACTS: One of Europe's most common small sharks; easily studied in aquariums; its skin was once used as a fine abrasive material known as "shark leather." Its distinctive egg cases often wash ashore, making them a familiar sight to beachgoers and divers.

Small-spotted catshark, *Scyliorhinus canicula*. Copyright © Lochlainn Seabrook.

SMOOTHHOUND SHARK

COMMON NAME: Smoothhound shark.

SCIENTIFIC NAME: *Mustelus mustelus* (Linnaeus, 1758).

FAMILY: Triakidae.

GROUP: Smoothhound sharks.

BIOLOGICAL STATUS: Living.

TIME ON EARTH: Approximately 30 million years.

GEOLOGIC AGE: Oligocene to present.

SIZE: Averages 4–5 ft; maximum about 6 ft; 25–53 lb.

HABITAT: Temperate and subtropical coastal waters, often near sandy or muddy bottoms.

DEPTH RANGE: Surface to about 1,300 ft.

GEOGRAPHIC RANGE: Eastern Atlantic from British Isles to South Africa, including the Mediterranean Sea.

DIET: Feeds on crustaceans, cephalopods, and small bony fish.

DISTINGUISHING FEATURES: Slender body, short snout, oval eyes, two dorsal fins of similar size, and smooth skin texture. Gray to brown dorsally with lighter underside.

ANATOMY & ADAPTATIONS: Possesses flattened molariform teeth for crushing hard-shelled prey. Well-developed lateral line enhances detection of bottom-dwelling organisms. Large pectoral fins allow stability and precise movement near the seafloor.

BEHAVIOR: Slow to moderate swimmer reaching about 8–10 mph. Gregarious, often forming schools. Active mainly at night, moving inshore to feed. Uses smell and electroreception to locate buried prey. Frequently rests motionless on the seafloor during daylight hours.

REPRODUCTION: Viviparous. Breeds in shallow coastal areas during spring and summer. Gestation lasts about 10–11 months; litters average 4–15 pups around 12 in. long. Females may reproduce only every other year.

PREDATORS: Larger sharks such as blue and mako sharks, and marine mammals including dolphins.

DANGER TO HUMANS: Harmless; avoids contact; no recorded attacks.

CONSERVATION STATUS: "Vulnerable." Threatened by overfishing, bycatch, and habitat degradation.

NOTABLE FACTS: Known for mild temperament and adaptability to aquaria. Its flesh, called "rock salmon," is commercially sold in Europe. Plays an important ecological role controlling crustacean populations and maintaining benthic balance.

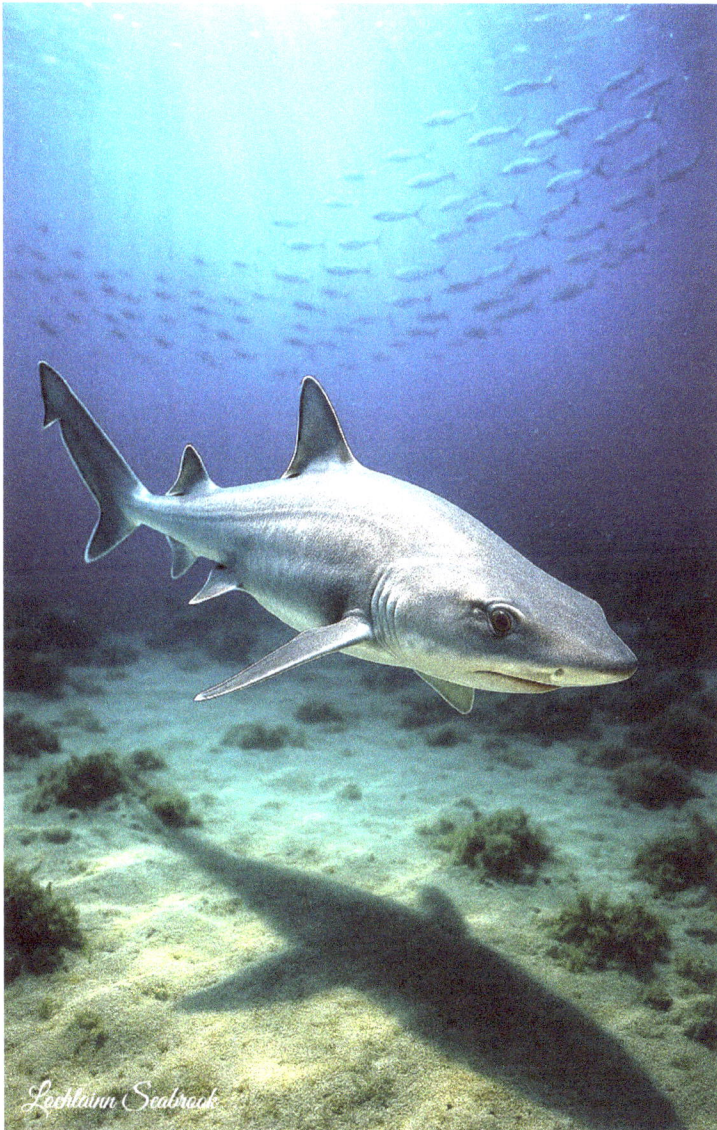

Smoothhound shark, *Mustelus mustelus*. Copyright © Lochlainn Seabrook.

SPINY DOGFISH

COMMON NAME: Spiny dogfish.

SCIENTIFIC NAME: *Squalus acanthias* (Linnaeus, 1758).

FAMILY: Squalidae.

GROUP: Dogfish sharks.

BIOLOGICAL STATUS: Living.

TIME ON EARTH: About 200 million years.

GEOLOGIC AGE: Early Jurassic to present.

SIZE: Average 3.3 ft; maximum 4.2 ft; 8–22 lb.

HABITAT: Temperate coastal and offshore waters, often over continental shelves.

DEPTH RANGE: Surface to 2,900 ft.

GEOGRAPHIC RANGE: Widely distributed in the North Atlantic, North Pacific, and Southern Hemisphere waters.

DIET: Small schooling fish, squid, shrimp, and crustaceans.

DISTINGUISHING FEATURES: Slim, gray body with white spots along the sides, narrow snout, and no anal fin. Two dorsal fins, each armed with a sharp, mildly venomous spine.

ANATOMY & ADAPTATIONS: Streamlined body suited for long migrations. Slow metabolism and efficient gill design allow endurance swimming in cool water. Uses electroreception and strong jaw muscles to capture swift prey. Liver rich in oil provides buoyancy. Venomous spines are defensive, capable of deterring larger predators.

BEHAVIOR: Forms large schools, often segregated by sex and size. Migrates seasonally in pursuit of prey and suitable temperature zones. Swims steadily at 2–4 mph, but can speed-burst faster when striking. Extremely social for a shark species; also highly migratory, sometimes traveling thousands of miles annually.

REPRODUCTION: Ovoviviparous; females give birth to 2–11 pups after an unusually long gestation of up to 24 months—the longest known among sharks.

PREDATORS: Larger sharks, seals, and orcas.

DANGER TO HUMANS: Harmless; occasionally inflicts minor punctures when handled.

CONSERVATION STATUS: "Vulnerable."

NOTABLE FACTS: Once the world's most abundant shark and heavily fished for food and oil. Females mature late, making populations slow to recover. Endurance and spines make it one of the ocean's most resilient sharks. Its lifespan—often exceeding 70 years—adds to its scientific importance.

Spiny dogfish, *Squalus acanthias*. Copyright © Lochlainn Seabrook.

SPOTTED WOBBEGONG

COMMON NAME: Spotted wobbegong.

SCIENTIFIC NAME: *Orectolobus maculatus* (Bonnaterre, 1788).

FAMILY: Orectolobidae.

GROUP: Wobbegongs.

BIOLOGICAL STATUS: Living.

TIME ON EARTH: About 11 million years.

GEOLOGIC AGE: Late Miocene to present.

SIZE: Average 6.5 ft; up to 10 ft; estimated 45–80 lb.

HABITAT: Coastal coral reefs, rocky reefs, and sandy bottoms.

DEPTH RANGE: Surface to about 360 ft.

GEOGRAPHIC RANGE: Western Pacific; mainly around southern Australia, from southern Queensland to southwestern Western Australia.

DIET: Bony fish, octopus, crabs, lobsters, and small sharks.

DISTINGUISHING FEATURES: Flat, broad head with complex skin lobes; mottled brown-and-yellow coloration forming symmetrical rosettes and blotches; large mouth extending behind eyes; ornate camouflage pattern ideal for ambush predation.

ANATOMY & ADAPTATIONS: Possesses dermal flaps that disrupt its outline and help lure prey; jaws equipped with small but sharp backward-curved teeth; capable of rapid suction strikes; cryptic patterning and low body profile provide excellent concealment on the seafloor.

BEHAVIOR: Nocturnal ambush predator; rests motionless by day, hunts at night; capable of sudden bursts of speed up to 5 mph; often remains in the same shelter for weeks; frequently rests on shallow reef ledges; commonly found on sandy bottoms beneath piers.

REPRODUCTION: Aplacental viviparous; gives birth to litters of 20–37 pups; young measure about 9–10 in at birth.

PREDATORS: Larger sharks, particularly great whites, and humans through fishing.

DANGER TO HUMANS: Generally docile but can bite if provoked or stepped on; holds tenaciously once latched.

CONSERVATION STATUS: Listed as "Least Concern" by the IUCN, but vulnerable to overfishing and habitat degradation.

NOTABLE FACTS: One of the largest wobbegong species; often found resting under ledges or wharves; sometimes kept in public aquariums due to its striking coloration and unique appearance; occasionally caught as bycatch in bottom trawls and used for meat and leather.

Spotted wobbegong, *Orectolobus maculatus*. Copyright © Lochlainn Seabrook.

SQUALICORAX

COMMON NAME: Squalicorax.
SCIENTIFIC NAME: *Squalicorax pristodontus* (Agassiz, 1843).
FAMILY: Anacoracidae.
GROUP: Mackerel sharks.
BIOLOGICAL STATUS: Extinct.
TIME ON EARTH: Late Cretaceous.
GEOLOGIC AGE: 100–66 million years ago.
SIZE: Up to 16 ft long; probably 500–1,500 lb.
HABITAT: Warm, shallow coastal and continental shelf waters.
DEPTH RANGE: Surface to about 650 ft.
GEOGRAPHIC RANGE: Global; fossils found in North America, Europe, Africa, Asia, and Antarctica.
DIET: Fish, marine reptiles, seabirds, and carrion.
DISTINGUISHING FEATURES: Broad triangular serrated teeth resembling those of a great white; robust body; short snout; deeply forked tail.
ANANTOMY & ADAPTATIONS: Teeth with fine serrations for slicing flesh and scavenging carcasses; strong jaws capable of removing large chunks of tissue; cartilaginous skeleton for speed and maneuverability; well-developed senses for detecting prey and carrion.
BEHAVIOR: Both predator and scavenger; evidence of feeding on mosasaurs and turtles; likely swam at moderate speeds around 15–20 mph while patrolling coasts; opportunistic feeder able to exploit diverse food sources.
REPRODUCTION: Probably gave birth to live young, like most lamniforms; young sharks were miniature versions of adults and grew quickly in warm Cretaceous seas.
PREDATORS: Large marine reptiles and bigger sharks such as the ancestors of *Cretoxyrhina* or *Carcharocles*.
DANGER TO HUMANS: None; extinct millions of years before humans appeared.
CONSERVATION STATUS: Extinct, known only from fossils.
NOTABLE FACTS: The Greco-Latin hybrid name *Squalicorax* means "shark raven," describing its scavenging behavior. Its serrated teeth are among the most common Cretaceous shark fossils. Bite marks matching *Squalicorax* teeth have been found on dinosaur bones, confirming its opportunistic feeding habits. Fossil evidence indicates it played a key ecological role as a scavenger or necrophage, and may have hunted in small groups.

Squalicorax, *Squalicorax pristodontus*. Copyright © Lochlainn Seabrook.

STETHACANTHUS

COMMON NAME: Stethacanthus (nickname, "iron-clad shark").
SCIENTIFIC NAME: *Stethacanthus altonensis* (St. John and Worthen, 1875).
FAMILY: Stethacanthidae.
GROUP: Stethacanthids.
BIOLOGICAL STATUS: Extinct.
TIME ON EARTH: Late Devonian to early Carboniferous.
GEOLOGIC AGE: 360–320 million years ago.
SIZE: Up to 6 ft long; estimated 20–100 lb.
HABITAT: Shallow warm seas over continental shelves and reef zones.
DEPTH RANGE: Surface to about 330 ft.
GEOGRAPHIC RANGE: North America, Europe, and Asia.
DIET: Small fish, cephalopods, and crustaceans.
DISTINGUISHING FEATURES: Flattened, anvil-shaped dorsal fin covered in denticles; blunt head; short snout; large pectoral fins; heterocercal tail; smooth-edged teeth.
ANATOMY & ADAPTATIONS: Had a cartilaginous skeleton typical of early sharks; large eyes for sight-based hunting; paired fins provided balance and lift; dorsal "brush" of denticles possibly used for display or hydrodynamic control; teeth adapted for gripping soft-bodied prey. Lateral line system helped detect vibrations in murky water.
BEHAVIOR: Likely a slow to moderate swimmer, cruising 5–10 mph. Probably moved alone or in small groups near reefs or sandy bottoms, ambushing prey from below. The dorsal brush was likely a male-only structure used in mating rituals or intimidation of rivals.
REPRODUCTION: Probably oviparous, laying eggs in shallow, protected areas.
PREDATORS: Larger sharks and early bony fish such as Cladoselache.
DANGER TO HUMANS: None; extinct long before humans.
CONSERVATION STATUS: Extinct.
NOTABLE FACTS: Stethacanthus is one of the earliest known true sharks. Its strange "ironing board" dorsal fin remains one of evolution's most unusual designs. Fossils from Ohio, Scotland, and Russia preserve skin impressions showing minute denticles. It represents an important transitional link between primitive cartilaginous fish and modern sharks.

Stethacanthus, *Stethacanthus altonensis*. Copyright © Lochlainn Seabrook.

SWELL SHARK

COMMON NAME: Swell shark.
SCIENTIFIC NAME: *Cephaloscyllium ventriosum* (Garman, 1880).
FAMILY: Scyliorhinidae.
GROUP: Catsharks.
BIOLOGICAL STATUS: Living.
TIME ON EARTH: ~35 million years.
GEOLOGIC AGE: Late Eocene to present.
SIZE: Commonly 2.5 to 3 ft; maximum 3.6 ft; weight 10–25 lb.
HABITAT: Rocky reefs, kelp forests, and sandy bottoms along continental shelves.
DEPTH RANGE: Surface to about 1,500 ft, most common between 16 and 500 ft.
GEOGRAPHIC RANGE: Eastern Pacific Ocean from central California to southern Mexico, including the Gulf of California.
DIET: Bony fish, crustaceans, mollusks, and cephalopods.
DISTINGUISHING FEATURES: Short, broad head; large oval eyes; catlike pupils; flattened body; brownish or yellowish coloration with dark blotches and saddle-shaped markings.
ANATOMY & ADAPTATIONS: Inflates its body with air or water to double its girth when threatened, lodging itself in reef crevices. Possesses small, sharp teeth and a tough skin with dermal denticles for protection. Nocturnal vision aided by vertical pupils and tapetum lucidum.
BEHAVIOR: Nocturnal ambush predator that spends the day resting in caves or under ledges and hunts slowly at night; swims at about 2–3 mph; curls into a U-shape when inflated to deter predators.
REPRODUCTION: Oviparous; females lay pairs of rectangular egg cases known as "mermaid's purses" that attach to kelp or rocks; incubation lasts 7–12 months depending on temperature. Hatchlings measure about 6 in at birth and are fully independent.
PREDATORS: Larger sharks, sea lions, and elephant seals.
DANGER TO HUMANS: Harmless; rarely bites; often handled by divers without incident.
CONSERVATION STATUS: "Least Concern."
NOTABLE FACTS: When captured it can emit a barking sound as air escapes from its stomach; frequently seen resting on the seafloor by divers off California. Sometimes observed sharing crevices with other swell sharks in groups. Its defensive inflation behavior inspired the genus name *Cephaloscyllium*, meaning "head cat."

Swell shark, *Cephaloscyllium ventriosum*. Copyright © Lochlainn Seabrook.

THRESHER SHARK

COMMON NAME: Thresher shark.
SCIENTIFIC NAME: *Alopias vulpinus* (Bonnaterre, 1788).
FAMILY: Alopiidae.
GROUP: Thresher sharks.
BIOLOGICAL STATUS: Living.
TIME ON EARTH: About 40 million years.
GEOLOGIC AGE: Eocene to present.
SIZE: Average 16 ft; maximum 20 ft; 250–1,100 lb.
HABITAT: Coastal and oceanic waters from surface to mid-depths.
DEPTH RANGE: Surface to about 1,800 ft.
GEOGRAPHIC RANGE: Worldwide in temperate and tropical seas, including the Atlantic, Pacific, and Indian Oceans.
DIET: Small schooling fish such as mackerel, herring, and sardines; also squid and crustaceans.
DISTINGUISHING FEATURES: Long upper tail lobe nearly equal to body length; large eyes; small mouth; pointed snout; crescent-shaped caudal fin.
ANATOMY & ADAPTATIONS: The elongated tail is used to whip and stun prey. Streamlined body, strong caudal muscles, and countershading enhance stealth and speed. Large pectoral fins improve control and lift. High red muscle content supports endurance during long chases. Heat-exchange vessels around the brain and eyes maintain reflexes in cold water.
BEHAVIOR: Solitary or in small groups. Uses tail to herd and strike prey. Can breach the surface. Fast swimmer reaching about 30 mph. Migratory and active during daylight. Known to encircle prey before striking with its tail, sometimes stunning multiple fish at once. Often travels long distances following seasonal shifts in prey abundance.
REPRODUCTION: Aplacental viviparous; embryos feed on unfertilized eggs. Litter of 2–4 pups about 5 ft long at birth. Mating thought to occur in offshore waters during summer.
PREDATORS: Larger sharks, orcas, and humans.
DANGER TO HUMANS: Shy and harmless; avoids divers.
CONSERVATION STATUS: "Vulnerable" from overfishing and bycatch.
NOTABLE FACTS: Named for its tail resembling a thresher's flail. Uses tail as a hunting tool. Prized by sport fishers and targeted commercially for meat and fins. A powerful jumper known to leap clear of the water when feeding or pursued.

Thresher shark, *Alopias vulpinus*. Copyright © Lochlainn Seabrook.

TIGER SHARK

COMMON NAME: Tiger shark.
SCIENTIFIC NAME: *Galeocerdo cuvier* (Péron and Lesueur, 1822).
FAMILY: Carcharhinidae.
GROUP: Requiem sharks.
BIOLOGICAL STATUS: Living.
TIME ON EARTH: About 23 million years.
GEOLOGIC AGE: Miocene to present.
SIZE: Commonly 10–14 ft; maximum recorded length 18 ft; males 850–1,400 lb; females 1,200–2,000 lb.
HABITAT: Coastal and pelagic tropical and subtropical waters worldwide.
DEPTH RANGE: Surface to about 3,000 ft, most often above 1,000 ft.
GEOGRAPHIC RANGE: Found in all major tropical and warm temperate seas, including the Atlantic, Pacific, and Indian Oceans, Gulf of America, and Caribbean Sea.
DIET: Highly opportunistic; consumes fish, rays, seabirds, turtles, marine mammals, and crustaceans.
DISTINGUISHING FEATURES: Broad, blunt snout; large mouth with heavy, serrated teeth; vertical dark stripes along sides (hence its common name) that fade with age; short but powerful body; distinct caudal fin with long upper lobe.
ANATOMY & ADAPTATIONS: Possesses serrated teeth ideal for slicing through bone, shell, and flesh. Liver rich in oil aids buoyancy. Excellent vision and electroreception assist in low light hunting. Spiral valve intestine slows digestion, allowing absorption of varied prey.
BEHAVIOR: Primarily nocturnal hunter. Solitary except during mating or feeding events. Slow-cruising but capable of sudden bursts up to 20 mph. Often patrols nearshore reefs and estuaries.
REPRODUCTION: Ovoviviparous. Gestation about 13–16 months. Produces litters of 10–80 pups, each about 2–3 ft at birth.
PREDATORS: Few natural enemies; large orcas may occasionally prey on juveniles.
DANGER TO HUMANS: Considered extremely dangerous; ranks second only to the great white in recorded attacks.
CONSERVATION STATUS: "Near Threatened." Populations declining due to bycatch and finning.
NOTABLE FACTS: Plays a key ecological role as a top predator controlling mid-level species.

Tiger shark, *Galeocerdo cuvier*. Copyright © Lochlainn Seabrook.

VELVET BELLY LANTERNSHARK

COMMON NAME: Velvet belly lanternshark.

SCIENTIFIC NAME: *Etmopterus spinax* (Linnaeus, 1758).

FAMILY: Etmopteridae.

GROUP: Lanternsharks.

BIOLOGICAL STATUS: Living.

TIME ON EARTH: About 60 million years.

GEOLOGIC AGE: Paleocene to present.

SIZE: Up to 2 ft in length; weight 1–4 lb.

HABITAT: Continental slopes and outer shelves of temperate and sub-Arctic seas.

DEPTH RANGE: 660–8,200 ft.

GEOGRAPHIC RANGE: Eastern Atlantic from Iceland to South Africa, including the Mediterranean Sea.

DIET: Bony fish, squid, shrimp, and small crustaceans.

DISTINGUISHING FEATURES: Compact, slender body with smooth, velvety, dark bluish-gray skin; pale lateral lines and distinctive light-emitting organs on the belly and fins. Short snout, large eyes, and small dorsal spines ahead of each fin.

ANATOMY & ADAPTATIONS: Possesses specialized photophores along the ventral surface that produce blue-green bioluminescence for camouflage and communication. Large green eyes enhance low-light vision. Dense dermal denticles reduce drag. Slow metabolism conserves energy in deep-sea conditions. Its liver is rich in squalene, improving buoyancy and pressure resistance.

BEHAVIOR: Nocturnal bottom dweller that forages individually or in loose groups. Uses counter-illumination to blend with faint down-welling light. Feeds slowly but efficiently, cruising at roughly 2 mph. Exhibits diel vertical migrations following prey movements. Shows mild territoriality around feeding zones.

REPRODUCTION: Ovoviviparous; females bear litters of 10–20 pups measuring about 6 in at birth. Gestation estimated near one year.

PREDATORS: Larger sharks and deep-sea fishes such as grenadiers and cod.

DANGER TO HUMANS: Harmless; too small to pose risk.

CONSERVATION STATUS: Listed as "Least Concern" by IUCN, but vulnerable to deep-water bycatch.

NOTABLE FACTS: The smallest known bioluminescent shark. Its light organs can be individually controlled through hormonal and nervous signals, making *Etmopterus spinax* one of the best-studied models of deep-sea bioluminescence among cartilaginous fish.

Velvet belly landternshark, *Etmopterus spinax*. Copyright © Lochlainn Seabrook.

WHALE SHARK

COMMON NAME: Whale shark.
SCIENTIFIC NAME: *Rhincodon typus* (Smith, 1828).
FAMILY: Rhincodontidae.
GROUP: Carpet sharks.
BIOLOGICAL STATUS: Living.
TIME ON EARTH: About 60 million years.
GEOLOGIC AGE: Paleocene to present.
SIZE: Up to 61.7 ft; 20,000–41,000 lb (up to 20.5 tons).
HABITAT: Warm, tropical, and subtropical oceans.
DEPTH RANGE: Surface to about 6,000 ft.
GEOGRAPHIC RANGE: Circumtropical; found in all major oceans between 30° N and 35° S latitude.
DIET: Plankton, krill, small fish, copepods, squid, and fish eggs filtered from the water.
DISTINGUISHING FEATURES: Enormous size, wide flattened head, terminal mouth, checkerboard pattern of light spots and stripes, large gill slits, crescent caudal fin.
ANATOMY & ADAPTATIONS: Possesses over 3,000 tiny teeth in several rows though largely unused for feeding. Uses suction and filter pads within gill rakers to strain microscopic prey. Thick skin, up to 4 in thick, provides protection. Broad dorsal and pectoral fins stabilize its slow cruising motion. Countershading provides concealment from both prey and predators.
BEHAVIOR: Solitary but sometimes aggregates at plankton blooms. Migratory, traveling thousands of miles annually. Swims slowly at 3 mph while filter-feeding near the surface. Gentle, docile, and tolerant of divers. No recorded attacks on humans.
REPRODUCTION: Ovoviviparous; females carry hundreds of fertilized eggs that hatch internally. Young born live at about 16–24 inches. Reproduction poorly understood.
PREDATORS: Few natural enemies; young may be taken by orcas, blue sharks, or large marlins.
DANGER TO HUMANS: Harmless; poses no threat except accidental contact due to size and weight.
CONSERVATION STATUS: "Endangered." Threatened by vessel strikes, entanglement, and illegal fin harvesting. Protected in many nations' waters.
NOTABLE FACTS: Individual spot patterns are unique, functioning like fingerprints for identification. Largest living fish species. Known to live more than 100 years.

Whale shark, *Rhincodon typus*. Copyright © Lochlainn Seabrook.

ZEBRA SHARK

COMMON NAME: Zebra shark.
SCIENTIFIC NAME: *Stegostoma tigrinum* (Forster, 1781).
FAMILY: Stegostomatidae.
GROUP: Carpet sharks.
BIOLOGICAL STATUS: Living.
TIME ON EARTH: About 30 million years.
GEOLOGIC AGE: Oligocene to present.
SIZE: Up to 8.9 ft; average 6.5 ft; 35–70 lb.
HABITAT: Warm coastal and coral reef environments.
DEPTH RANGE: 16–200 ft, occasionally deeper.
GEOGRAPHIC RANGE: Tropical Indo-Pacific from South Africa and the Red Sea to Australia and the western Pacific.
DIET: Mollusks, crustaceans, small bony fish, and sea snakes.
DISTINGUISHING FEATURES: Long, flexible body; broad, flattened head; small mouth set forward; prominent ridges along flanks; long tail nearly as long as the body; striking juvenile stripes that change to adult spots.
ANATOMY & ADAPTATIONS: Possesses small barbels for sensing prey, strong crushing jaws, and nasal grooves aiding respiration while resting. Pectoral fins are large and rounded for stability among coral. Its spotted skin provides camouflage against reef substrates. Able to gulp air for short periods to adjust buoyancy in shallow waters.
BEHAVIOR: Slow-moving, nocturnal bottom-dweller that rests on sand or reef ledges by day and hunts at night. Solitary except when breeding or feeding in groups. Uses undulating body motion to maneuver through tight reef crevices. Maximum recorded speed about 2 mph. Occasionally visits cleaning stations where small fish, such as cleaner wrasses and cleaner gobies, remove parasites.
REPRODUCTION: Oviparous; females lay large, dark egg cases that hatch after roughly 5–6 months. Hatchlings are banded, resembling juvenile coloration patterns.
PREDATORS: Larger sharks and marine mammals.
DANGER TO HUMANS: Harmless; rarely displays defensive behavior.
CONSERVATION STATUS: Endangered due to overfishing, habitat loss, and aquarium collection.
NOTABLE FACTS: Named for its juvenile stripes, which fade into spots as it matures. Plays a key role in coral reef ecosystems by regulating invertebrate populations.

Zebra shark, *Stegostoma tigrinum*. Copyright © Lochlainn Seabrook.

The End

SEA RAVEN PRESS

Artisan-Crafted Books & Merch From the Rocky Mountains

MEET THE AUTHOR

LOCHLAINN SEABROOK is a prolific lifelong researcher, historian, author, artist, and composer whose knowledge and experience span numerous fields. His remarkable productivity stems from his broad interests, decades of meticulous research, and an unwavering daily devotion to writing and creative exploration.

The idea of specializing in a single subject is a modern invention. In the spirit of the great polymaths—Aristotle, Isaac Newton, Benjamin Franklin, and Thomas Jefferson—Seabrook works across dozens of disciplines, with intellectual pursuits encompassing history, science, philosophy, religion, and the arts. The result is an expansive body of original writings that distill years of careful analysis into clear, accessible language for the general reader.

Rejecting the narrow confines of modern specialization, Seabrook views all knowledge as intrinsically interconnected. This integrative vision, combined with long hours of focused, solitary study and a rigorous work ethic, has enabled him to produce an extraordinary corpus of literature uniting the sciences and the humanities—a natural outgrowth of a lifetime devoted to inquiry, creativity, and the preservation of evidence-based history.

AMERICAN POLYMATH LOCHLAINN SEABROOK is a bestselling author, award-winning historian, and acclaimed multidisciplinary artist. A descendant of the families of Alexander Hamilton Stephens, John Singleton Mosby, Edmund Winchester Rucker, and William Giles Harding, the neo-Victorian scholar is a 7th generation Kentuckian, and one of the most prolific and widely read traditional writers in the world today. Known by literary critics as the "new Shelby Foote," the "American Robert Graves," the "Southern Joseph Campbell," and the "Rocky Mountain Richard Jefferies," and by his fans as the "the best author ever," he is a recipient of the United Daughters of the Confederacy's prestigious Jefferson Davis Historical Gold Medal, and is considered the foremost Southern interpreter of American Civil War history—or what he refers to as the War for the Constitution (1861-1865).

A lifelong litterateur, the Sons of Confederate Veterans member has authored and edited books ranging in topics from ancient and modern history, politics, science, comparative religion, diet and nutrition, spirituality, astronomy, entertainment, military, biography, mysticism, anthropology, cryptozoology, photography, and Bible studies, to natural history, technology, paleography, music, humor, gastronomy, etymology, paleontology, onomastics, mysteries, alternative health and fitness, wildlife, alternate history, comparative mythology, genealogy, Christian history, and the paranormal; books that his readers describe as "game changers," "transformative," and "life altering."

One of America's most popular living historians, nature writers, and Transcendentalists, he is a 17th generation Southerner of Appalachian heritage who descends from dozens of patriotic Revolutionary War soldiers and Confederate soldiers from Kentucky, Tennessee, North Carolina, and Virginia. Also a history, wildlife, and nature preservationist, the well-respected scrivener began life as a child prodigy, later maturing into an archetypal Renaissance Man.

Besides being cofounder and co-CEO of Sea Raven Press, an accomplished writer, author, historian, biographer, lexicographer, encyclopedist, neologist, publisher, editor, poet, polymathic creative, onomastician, etymologist, and Bible authority, the influential prosateur is also a Kentucky Colonel, eagle scout, entrepreneur, businessman, composer, screenwriter, nature, wildlife, and landscape photographer, videographer, and filmmaker, artist, artisan, painter, watercolorist, sculptor, ceramic artist, visual artist, sketch artist, pen and ink artist, graphic artist, graphic designer, book designer, book formatter, editorial designer, book cover designer, publishing designer, Web designer, poster artist, digital artist, cartoonist, content creator, inventor, aquarist, genealogist, ufologist, jewelry designer, jewelry maker, former history museum docent, teacher's assistant, and a former Red Cross certified lifeguard, ranch hand, zookeeper, and wrangler. A contemporary songwriter (of some 3,000 songs in a dozen genres), he is also a pianist, organist, drummer, bass player, rhythm guitarist, rhythm mandolinist, percussionist, electronic musician, synthesist, clavichordist, harpsichordist, classical composer, jingle composer, film composer (currently his musical work has been featured in 11 movies), lyricist, band leader, multi-instrument musician, lead vocalist, backup vocalist, session player, music producer, and recording studio mixing engineer, who has worked and performed with some of Nashville's top musicians and singers.

Currently Seabrook is the multi-genre author and editor of over 100 adult and children's books (totaling some 30,000 pages and 15,000,000 words) that have earned him accolades from around the globe. His works, which have sold on every continent except Antarctica, have introduced hundreds of thousands to vital facts that have been left out of our mainstream books. He has been endorsed internationally by leading experts, museum curators, award-winning historians, chart-topping authors, celebrities, filmmakers, noted scientists, well regarded educators, TV show hosts and producers, renowned military artists, venerable heritage organizations, and distinguished academicians of all races, creeds, and colors.

He currently holds two interesting world records: He is the author of the most books on American military officer Nathan Bedford Forrest, and he was the first to publicize and describe the 19th-Century platform reversal of America's two main political parties, namely that Civil War era Democrats (primarily in the South—the Confederacy) were Conservatives, while Civil War era Republicans (primarily in the North—the Union) were Liberals.

Of northern, western, and central European ancestry, he is the 6th great-grandson of the Earl of Oxford and a descendant of European royalty through his Kentucky father and West Virginia mother. A proud descendant of Appalachian coal miners, trainmen, mountain folk, and wilderness pioneers, his modern day cousins include: Johnny Cash, Elvis Presley, Lisa Marie Presley, Billy Ray and Miley Cyrus, Patty Loveless, Tim McGraw, Lee Ann Womack, Dolly Parton, Pat Boone, Naomi, Wynonna, and Ashley Judd, Ricky Skaggs, the Sunshine Sisters, Martha Carson, Chet Atkins, Patrick J. Buchanan, Cindy Crawford, Bertram Thomas Combs (Kentucky's 50th governor), Edith Bolling (second wife of President Woodrow Wilson), Andy Griffith, Riley Keough, George C. Scott, Robert Duvall, Reese Witherspoon, Lee Marvin, Rebecca Gayheart, and Tom Cruise.

A constitutionalist, avid outdoorsman, wilderness conservationist, and gun rights advocate, Seabrook is the author of the international blockbuster, *Everything You Were Taught About the Civil War is Wrong, Ask a Southerner!* He lives with his wife and family in the magnificent Rocky Mountains, heart of the American West, where you will find him writing, hiking, and filming.

For more information on Mr. Seabrook visit

LOCHLAINNSEABROOK.COM

Praise for Author-Historian-Artist
Lochlainn Seabrook

"Bestselling author, award-winning historian, and esteemed nature writer Lochlainn Seabrook straddles multiple genres with ease, seamlessly weaving together history, science, politics, philosophy, and spirituality with the authority of a scholar and the flair of a storyteller." — SEA RAVEN PRESS

COMMENTS FROM OUR READERS AROUND THE WORLD

✻ "Lochlainn Seabrook is a genius writer!" — STEVEN WARD

✻ "Best author ever." — EMILY

✻ "We get asked a lot what books we use and read. We don't do many modern historians, but we make an exception for some, and Lochlainn Seabrook is one of them. His works are completely well researched from original documents, and heavily footnoted and documented." — SOUTHERN HISTORICAL SOCIETY

✻ "Looking forward to more Lochlainn Seabrook books, my favourite historian!" — ALBERTO IGLESIAS

✻ "Lochlainn Seabrook is one of the finest authors on true history in this century. His books should be on every student's desk." — RONDA SAMMONS RENO

✻ "All of Col. Seabrook's books are great. I have bought most of them and want to end up buying them all." — DAVID VAUGHN

✻ "Lochlainn pulls together such arcane facts with relative ease, compiling these into ordinary prose that strike to the heart with substance, no fluff-speak. I am awestruck! Really. He is an inspiration to me. . . . He is truly a revolutionist. He dares to speak what others whisper; he writes with a boldness and an authoritative knowledge that is second to none." — JAY KRUIZENGA

✻ "Mr. Lochlainn Seabrook is . . . the most well researched and heavily documented author I've ever read. His books are must haves. Everything he writes should be required reading! I assure you, you won't be disappointed. One simply cannot go wrong with his books. Mr. Seabrook is awesome! . . . I have never read any other author as well researched and footnoted as him. I've been in love with Mr. Seabrook for almost 5 years now. His quick wit and logic is enough reason to purchase his books. But the mere fact that he's so extensively researched is icing on the cake. Mr. Seabrook is my favorite, hands down." — LANI BURNETTE RINKEL

✻ "My favorite book is the Bible. Lochlainn Seabrook wrote my second favorite book." — RICHARD FINGER

✻ "I have a new favorite author and his name is Lochlainn Seabrook." — J. EWING

✻ "Lochlainn Seabrook is an incredible writer and I love all of his books on the South. . . . His writing is brilliant. . . . I look forward to reading more of his masterpieces. Thank you." — JOEY

✻ "It's hard to choose just one of Lochlainn's books!" — ROSANNE STEELE

✻ "Mr. Seabrook, thank you ever so much for blessing us with your most enlightening works." — LAURENCE DRURY

✻ "I recommend anything written by Lochlainn Seabrook." — HOTRODMOB

✻ "Awesome books . . . by a great writer of truth, Lochlainn. Thank you so much. Keep up the great work you do." — WILDBUNCH19INF

✻ "I love Lochlainn Seabrook's style and approach. It's not the 'norm.' What a miracle his books are. . . . He is a literal life changing author! Amazing books!" — KEITH PARISH

✯ "I adore Mr. Seabrook's style and I love his books. I love an author that does proper research, and still finds a way to engage the reader. Mr. Seabrook does an admirable job of both." — DONALD CAUL

✯ "Lochlainn Seabrook's books are much more well researched and authoritative than those eminently celebrated as being the authorities on the subjects he writes on. You can always trust to find the truth in his writings. . . . He does not rewrite history, but instead shows it as it is." — GARY STIER

✯ "I love all of Colonel Seabrook's books. They are informative and enlightening, and his warm Southern hospitality writing style makes you feel right at home." — KEITH CRAVEN

✯ "Lochlainn Seabrook's work is an absolute treasure of scholarship and historic scope." — MARK WAYNE CUNNINGHAM

✯ "Mr. Seabrook's command of . . . history is breathtaking. . . . He deserves great renown—check out his books!" — MARGARET SIMMONS

✯ "I love Seabrook's writings. LOVE!!! . . . So grateful to know the truth! Keep writing Lochlainn!!!" — REBECCA DALRYMPLE

✯ "Lochlainn Seabrook . . . [has] probably [written] the best book on mental science in existence by a living author. Along with Thomas Troward, Emmet Fox, and Jack Addington, Mr. Seabrook is one of the top four mental science authors of all time, since biblical times." - IAN BARTON STEWART

✯ "Glad I discovered Mr. Seabrook! . . . He writes eye opening books! Unbelievable the facts he unearths - and he backs it all up with truth, notes, footnotes, and bibliography! . . . He always amazes me! His books always see the whole picture. His timelines and bibliographies are incredible. He always provides carefully reasoned arguments! He's the best. To me I think he's better than the late great Shelby Foote! America needs more like Lochlainn Seabrook. I can't wait to own all of his books on the war someday. Everyone who wants the Truth, who seeks the Truth and wants the full story, should read his books." — JOHN BULL BADER

✯ "I love all of Colonel Seabrook's books!" — DEBBIE SIDLE

✯ "Amazing books for unreconstructed people who actually want to know the TRUTH. Seabrook's skill in writing and researching has no equal since the great Shelby Foote. If I could rate his books more than five stars I would." — CANDICE

✯ "Lochlainn Seabrook is well educated and versed in what he writes and I'm impressed with the delivery." — THOMAS L. WHITE

✯ "Lochlainn Seabrook is the author of great works of scholarship." — JOHN B.

✯ "Thank you Lochlainn Seabrook for your wonderful books! You are the real deal! You are an amazing author and I love your books!!" — SOPHIA MEOW CELLIST

✯ "I really enjoy Mr. Seabrook's books! His knowledge is beyond belief!" — SANDRA FISH

✯ "Love Lochlainn Seabrook. Awesome!!" — ROBIN HENDERSON ARISTIDES

✯ "Kudos to Lochlainn Seabrook who is a very good and informative professional truthful historian. We need more like him!" — AMY VACHON

Nurture Your Mind, Body, and Spirit!

READ THE BOOKS OF

SEA RAVEN PRESS

Visit our Webstore for a wide selection of wholesome, family-friendly, evidence-based, educational books for all ages. You'll be glad you did!

ARTISAN-CRAFTED BOOKS & MERCH FROM THE ROCKY MOUNTAINS

THANK YOU FOR SUPPORTING OUR SMALL AMERICAN FAMILY BUSINESS!

SeaRavenPress.com

Visit our sister sites:
LochlainnSeabrook.com
YouTube.com/user/SeaRavenPress
YouTube.com/@SeabrookFilms
Rumble.com/user/SeaRavenPress
Pond5.com/artist/LochlainnSeabrook

A school of scalloped hammerhead sharks (*Sphyrna lewini*) glides gracefully through the sunlit waters of the Gulf of America. Copyright © Lochlainn Seabrook.

If you enjoyed this book you will be interested in some of Colonel Seabrook's popular related titles:

☛ WHEN MONSTERS RULED: THE 25 SCARIEST ANIMALS OF THE PREHISTORIC WORLD
☛ NORTH AMERICA'S AMAZING MAMMALS: AN ENCYCLOPEDIA FOR THE WHOLE FAMILY
☛ THE CONCISE BOOK OF OWLS: A GUIDE TO NATURE'S MOST MYSTERIOUS BIRDS
☛ ROCKY MOUNTAIN EQUINES: A PHOTOGRAPHIC COLLECTION OF HORSES, DONKEYS, AND MULES OF THE AMERICAN WEST
☛ ROCKY MOUNTAIN BISON: A PHOTOGRAPHIC COLLECTION OF BISON OF THE AMERICAN WEST
☛ THE CRYPTID FILES UNSEALED: AN ILLUSTRATED GUIDE TO THE WORLD'S MOST TERRIFYING UNKNOWN CREATURES
☛ THE CONCISE BOOK OF TIGERS: A GUIDE TO NATURE'S MOST REMARKABLE CATS

Available from Sea Raven Press and wherever fine books are sold

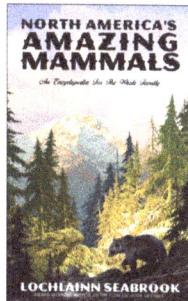

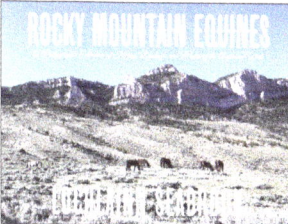

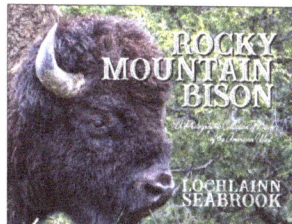

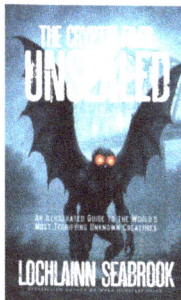

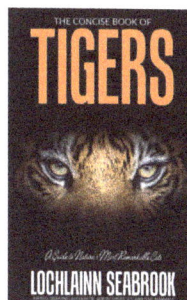

PLEASE VISIT OUR WEBSTORE FOR A COMPLETE LIST OF COLONEL SEABROOK'S BOOKS, AS WELL AS HIS FINE ART NATURE & WILDLIFE PHOTO PRINTS, WALL POSTERS, AND BUMPER STICKERS

SeaRavenPress.com

www.ingramcontent.com/pod-product-compliance
Lightning Source LLC
Chambersburg PA
CBHW040136270326
41927CB00019B/3402

* 9 7 8 1 9 5 5 3 5 1 7 2 0 *